Loving Practice,
Developing Discipline

Loving Practice, Developing Discipline

A Parent's Guide to Turning Music Lessons into Life Lessons

Dr. Klondike Steadman

First Edition, June 2019, manufactured in USA
1 2 3 4 5 6 7 8 9 10 LSI 19 20 22 23 24 25
Set in Cochin, Gils San, Garamond

International Standard Book Number: 978-0-9994978-6-9

All illustrations by Tracy Sullivan at Project by Project.

All photos are individually attributed to the authors.

Cover photo of Jeremiah used by permission of The Bolke Family.

Orpheus Academy of Music
3918 Far West Blvd, Ste C
Austin, TX 78731
www.orpheusacademy.com

CONTENTS

Dedicated to my daughter, Mei Yin.

ACKNOWLEDGMENTS

I would like to thank my wife, Wendy, for teaching me so much about how to create space for new ideas and for encouraging me to actually jump off the cliff, take a year off from work, and actually write this thing (rather than just talking about it all the time).

I would also like to thank all the parents who shared their struggles, triumphs, ideas, and questions with me, but especially Jay, who is just amazing in all ways (as a parent, musician, student, proofreader...). To Chelsea, Jeanette and Johnathan for the endless edits — you taught me that even those who struggle with writing can write a book. Thank you Kari and Satheesh for the use of your beautiful secluded cabin where I could write distraction-free: It turns out that being thoughtful about where to practice is just as important in writing as it is in music. Of course, most of this book is largely based on what my guitar students have shared with me about what has worked for them (and what hasn't). And to the students and faculty of Orpheus Academy of Music who have shared through surveys, discussion groups, and more — this book would not exist without you! A huge thank you to ALL OF YOU.

To the incredible concert artists, Adam Holzman, Anton Nel, and Gregory Allen, who each took me on a tour of his musical childhood and opened his life to me: Thank you! — Time is more than money: It is the stuff of life. And the same goes double for my mentor in education, Dr. Robert Duke, who has sat with me, encouraged me, and opened my eyes to entirely new ways of thinking about what it is we do when we engage in this act called "learning."

Above all, I would like to thank my daughter, Mei Yin: You continue to teach me to be a better teacher, a better dad, and a better listener. I hope that trying out these practice tips on you has not scarred you for life, or at least, if it has, you will eventually forgive me...

FOREWORD

Making music is a tremendously rewarding activity, one that engages more of the human brain than just about anything else we do. Music and all of the arts are deeply baked into human culture, as they embody fundamental aspects of human communication and expression. To teach children about the arts is to teach them about the cultures and societies in which they live, while at the same time helping them develop sophisticated skills in auditory and visual discrimination, fine motor skills, and a sense of personal accomplishment through active participation in meaningful creative endeavors. And, if one needs a more practical rationale for music study, there is no better activity through which children can observe a tangible relationship between their own efforts and the results their efforts produce (in terms of increased skill, capacity, and expressive potential) than learning to sing or play an instrument.

To participate successfully in active music-making is one of the great joys of the human experience. Throughout history, children beginning in infancy have watched and listened to older and more experienced music-makers, and they have aspired and tried and practiced and tried some more, all the while expending effort and precious attention to make music themselves. Some of these aspirations and efforts resulted in successful outcomes. Others, not so much. The path to developing music skills under any circumstance is rather messy and nonlinear. What caring, skillful parents and teachers do is create pathways for learning that deftly weave together strategic experiences that generate appropriate challenges, set up moments of meaningful accomplishment, and lead to increasing levels of independence.

Consider a young child sitting at the piano, as she does on most weekdays, practicing exercises and pieces for her lesson. She struggles mightily to perfect a passage from a Mozart sonata with an awkward fingering, playing the figure slowly at first, then gradually faster until she performs it correctly in several consecutive repetitions.

She's more attentive and her efforts are more concentrated than in just about any other intellectual or physical activity in which she participates. When she finally is able to negotiate the passage, she plays through the entire movement with a musical character that reflects her feelings of pleasure, having recognized that her efforts have led to a tangible accomplishment. What explains this child's focus, concentration, extended effort, expression of ineffable emotion, and sense of personal satisfaction and accomplishment?

Perhaps it is her love of music in general, her love of Mozart in particular, her desire to please her teacher or her parents, or her desire to perform well on an upcoming recital. More likely, it's some combination of all of these. Such potentially powerful motivators don't arise in a vacuum, but are the result of the concerted and thoughtful efforts of attentive, caring adults who fill the child's environment with the sounds of music, facilitate individual study with excellent teachers, provide meaningful and appropriate performance experiences, and tangibly convey their own love of music.

We know that music practice by the most skilled performers comprises a suite of essential features: thoughtful musical intention, deliberate approaches to problem solving, performing during practice with expressive inflection. We also know that most beginners don't practice like that, not because they can't, but because they've not been adequately prepared to do so. Learners must be able to distinguish one repetition from another, and as they gain in physical skill, there must be commensurate gains in auditory and physical discrimination. Practicing is not fruitful if students can't hear or feel the difference between one repetition and the next. If they can't, it's not surprising that practicing is viewed as generally unmotivating because, literally, it's all the same to them.

So how do some children develop into expert learners and persist in music study over time, while others face seemingly insurmountable obstacles, mind-numbing boredom, and a passionate desire to escape the unrelenting drudgery of practice? There are certainly some genetic predispositions at play. Some children are more patient than others, others more anxious, others more driven. But none of these predispositions are determinative. All children have the capacity to learn and enjoy the ins and outs of acquiring skill and understanding.

Though their learning tempos may vary, they all can arrive at wonderful destinations, given the right guidance and support. Parents and teachers provide the environments in which children's interests are nurtured and their aspirations come to fruition, instilling effective habits of thinking and doing—effective habits of learning.

Children don't come into the world like new cars direct from the factory of a single manufacturer. Although they tend to work in fundamentally similar ways, they are far from identical. Creating environments conducive to their growth, environments that are likely to inspire interest in the arts and to develop the habits of thinking and behavior required to reach the goals they set for themselves, is one of the many daunting challenges that confront every parent. There are no simple recipes, of course, but we can learn from the experiences of successful people who have not only invested in the well-being of children—their own and others'—but who have also thought a great deal about how all of this happens and are able to express in clear language what it means and what it takes to be a loving guide to a loved child.

Klondike Steadman, whose work as an artist, teacher, and thinker I have long admired, has created something wonderful and meaningful in *Loving Practice, Developing Discipline*. There's insight and wisdom here that can only come from a perceptive, focused mind with a tenacious devotion to the flourishing of children—in the arts and in life.

Robert Duke, PhD
Austin, TX

Robert Duke is the Marlene and Morton Meyerson Centennial Professor and Head of Music and Human Learning at The University of Texas at Austin. He is the author of *Intelligent Music Teaching: Essays on the Core Principles of Effective Instruction*, *The Habits of Musicianship*, which he co-authored with Jim Byo of Louisiana State University, and *Brain Briefs*, which he co-authored with Art Markman, his co-host on the public radio program and podcast *Two Guys on Your Head*, produced by KUT Radio in Austin.

1

INTRODUCTION

"I need a red crayon and some paper," my daughter says.

"You need a what? It's 2:50. The concert starts in 10 minutes," I say, trying to stay calm. This is her first "Home Concert" (a performance of 12 short pieces for a gathering of family and friends), and I am clearly more nervous about it than she is.

"I need a red crayon. I want to write a story about how I learned guitar, so people can read it."

"Um … Okay, here. I'll go tell the guests to hang on a moment."

She proceeds to write a four-page, illustrated "book" about her first year in guitar, folds it, and hands it out to the audience to read while she performs.

The concert goes well. She is a little tight, not as expressive as usual, but is focused and plays solidly. As her accompanist, I am so nervous that I forget that we decided she would do "Kom Se Mari," a Korean folk song, as a solo, and I play along with her, despite her whispers and glares while we are playing. In the end, the concert is a huge success, the audience of seven close friends give her a standing ovation, rave about her book, and I can see the joy in her expression as she takes her bows. She and her friends all eat cookies then go play in the creek and, laughing, get totally soaked.

To this day, that is one of the happiest moments of my life. While it has faded somewhat in her memory, it remained a highlight for her as well for quite some

Mei Yin's Home Concert
Photo courtesy of Jim Garrison

time — until she started doing bigger things in music. That day I learned in a very powerful way that, even for five-year-olds, music is about telling a story. People of all ages want to say something meaningful with their art, and for her, it was the story of how she learned guitar.

Cover of Mei Yin's story book

This book is mostly about the lessons I have learned from my daughter, from my students, and from my own journey in learning to play the guitar. I have tried to be as exhaustive as I could in researching the subjects of practice, discipline, and learning, and I have benefited tremendously from the input of other teachers, performers, and parents. In the end, though, it is always the lessons from direct experience that resonate most powerfully. I am certain the same will be true for you.

℘

The opportunity to develop musical talent is one of the best gifts you can give your child. From personal expression, to sharing the joy of music through performance, to brain development, to the benefits of being in a band, to the deep connection formed with one's cultural heritage, music yields incalculable rewards to those who pursue it. But of course, you knew all that, or you wouldn't be reading this book in the first place.

The problem every parent runs into sooner or later is that developing into a true musician is hard. So hard, in fact, that most people want to give up somewhere along the way (maybe multiple places along the way). Sometimes it is the child who wants to quit, and sometimes it is the parent. Sometimes both. And this is *completely normal*, because making music is one of the few activities that intensely challenges us physically, mentally, and emotionally — all at the same time. It challenges us physically to develop amazing dexterity; it challenges us intellectually to understand complex patterns of sound, the notation symbols that represent those sounds, the complex history and cultural significance of the music; and, most of all, it challenges us emotionally and even spiritually to perform the music in a way that expresses our own individuality. I often say that performing music well is like playing football while taking a math test and giving the acting performance of our lives. To play even one simple song beautifully demands our entire being to be engaged. So, as any professional musician will tell you, sooner or later you are going to want to quit. I can remember being so frustrated at times that I wanted to throw my guitar through my bedroom window.

The good news is that this intense difficulty may itself be the most valuable benefit that music has to offer. The very fact that something so intrinsically rewarding is so difficult gives us the opportunity and motivation to develop the character traits that lead to great success and happiness in life: *Discipline, curiosity, grit,* and, ultimately, the skill to transform ourselves through practice.

This book is about how our children can learn to understand themselves and their own internal motivators to make the challenging process of becoming a musician a joyful journey. If we can teach our children to engage in learning such a complex skill as music in ways that work for them, we will have given them one of the most powerful assets of all: self-knowledge.

As a teacher and a parent, my deepest aim is for my daughter and all my students to become happier, more successful human beings. Whether they pursue music professionally or some other career is irrelevant; if music helps them develop the life skills to handle the inevitable hardships and difficulties as well as the opportunities and triumphs that life presents, then I am happy to have been a part of that development.

Different Paths

When I turned 10, a friend of my father's gave me my dad's old guitar, which he had held onto after my father had died. Since I had hardly known my father, I immediately took to the instrument and found a neighbor who played a little and would accept trading an hour of work for an hour of instruction in classical guitar. My parents' engagement with my musical studies was minimal at best. On the one hand, they often took me to parties where folk singing was the center of the evening, and I quickly developed a sense that being musical was a source of joy. On the other hand, as my obsession with practicing classical guitar grew, there was very little support or even interest from my parents. In spite of this (or perhaps because of it!), I became increasingly obsessed with practicing as much as possible. Music was simultaneously an escape from some very traumatic circumstances, a means of self-expression, and a source of identity and self-esteem.

My wife, Wendy, never asked for piano lessons, but when she turned four, a piano showed up in her house in Jiayi, Taiwan, and thereafter she was assigned to an hour a day of practice, under the watchful eye of her mother or grandmother. She liked her teacher and some of the music, but the emphasis from her parents was on excelling compared to her peers. There was little or no praise, and any resistance to practice was met with punishment. Nevertheless, as her skill grew, so did her love of music, and eventually she chose to combine her love of helping others with her love of music, and she became a piano teacher.

While neither of us had anything resembling the kind of support that we would encourage parents of our own students to provide, somehow we both ended up loving music and learning important life skills from our musical studies. As a teacher and as a parent of a musical child, I frequently remind myself of three things:

1. **Every musical journey is unique.**
2. **"Perfect parenting" is not required.**
3. **The life benefits of music are vast, powerful, and available to all, regardless of their background.**

The purposes of this book are (1) to offer some suggestions to make the journey more joyful and more fruitful and (2) to transfer those experiences to all areas of your child's development. It is decidedly not an instructional manual on the one right way to raise musical children. In fact, the idea that there is a right and wrong way to go about helping your child practice is probably one of the greatest sources of difficulty for parents of musical children. The anxiety that emanates from trying to raise perfect little musicians is counterproductive to making music and can be destructive to family relations. There are infinite joyful approaches to this process, and there are equally infinite ways to recover from losing touch with our intention of making music a joyful part of our child's development.

The True Benefits of Music

In 1993, Rauscher, Shaw, and Ky published an article in *Nature* that investigated the effect of listening to Mozart's music on spatial reasoning abilities. Despite the fact that the study found only a temporary effect on spatial reasoning (it never dealt with I.Q.), the media and music lovers everywhere jumped at the opportunity to suggest that listening to music makes you smarter. Ever since, reports of the amazing power of music to transform our thinking and develop the brains of our children have shown up with increasing regularity in our newspapers, magazines, morning television talk shows, and now our Facebook feeds.

I would suggest that there is no need to rely on shaky evidence of some kind of magical and ephemeral effect of music on the brain: The real benefits are manifestly powerful and easily witnessed every day. Here are just a few benefits that parents commonly tell me they see in their children:

Creativity and Self-Expression

Parents consistently tell me that among their highest priorities for their children is that they gain the ability to express themselves through music. Some parents say they wish they had had the opportunity to learn; others say that music saved their lives in a difficult time or brought them joy; nearly all recognize this as the primary reason for learning an instrument. In my own teaching, getting to know my students personally so that together we can find music that expresses their unique personality is not only key to keeping them motivated, but also integral to their development as a whole person. One of my students delights in using his guitar as part of his Hindu prayer practice. Others, such as my daughter, are interested in flashier pieces with lots of technical difficulties. Many of my students enjoy music connected to games they love to play or happy experiences: The younger students delight in playing "Ring around the Rosie" or "Jingle Bells." As they grow older, many want to learn the songs in their video games.

Unfortunately, too often children are told that they must "master the basics" before they can begin to express themselves musically. In fact, a personal connection to the music is the best way to engage with learning the basics. Most children are as eager to improvise and compose within the first year of music study as they are to write stories in kindergarten. Not only does this stoke their creativity, it also provides motivation to practice and an opportunity to learn so much about music.

As a parent, you can help your child find her personal expression by asking her which pieces are her favorites, and why. When she performs a piece in a way clearly satisfying to her, let her know how much joy you hear in her playing. Look for a teacher who recognizes the importance of self-expression from the very beginning, and share your child's interests with her teacher.

Social Development and Teamwork

Music is a form of social communication and bonding. Learning music gives us the opportunity to participate in musical ensembles such as bands, orchestras, choirs, as well as small chamber music ensembles. When well-run, these groups provide an opportunity to learn to work well with others, be part of something bigger than ourselves, connect with our peers, and learn to benefit from peer pressure to perform at higher standards.

For myself and for many of my students, being part of an ensemble has been one of the most powerful and motivating experiences of our lives. My jazz band in high school both challenged me and transformed me as a player. Many of the other kids were already at a professional level and did not accept anything less than the highest level of playing from other band members. It was difficult for me to raise my playing even to an acceptable level, but the process was transformative.

At Orpheus Academy of Music, which my wife and I established, playing in ensembles is a core part of every student's experience. We notice that students are often willing to practice harder to prepare for ensemble rehearsal and performances than for any other reason. When rehearsals are conducted in a supportive manner, the students learn to listen, respond, and assist their fellow members with kindness and intelligence, with truly powerful results.

Physical Development

Music is one of the few activities that engages every part of the brain. The fine motor skills and muscular development required to play an instrument well is so intense that it is among the rare skills resulting in visible changes on brain scans.

It is always a delight to see a student go from struggling to even identify and move each individual finger independently, to finding that they can control those same fingers to play a melody, to finally being able to effortlessly perform a passage of extreme beauty and complexity. Just the other day, my daughter was playing a passage requiring blinding speed, with exceptional control and expression. When I said, "That's amazing. I wish I could play that passage that well," her response was, "Well, it should sound good. I practically wore my fingertips off practicing it."

Mathematical and Scientific Understanding

Personally, I am not convinced that studying music has a greater effect on mathematical abilities than, say, getting a math tutor. However, it certainly provides ample opportunity to strengthen those skills in an artistic context. Ratios and fractions must be internalized and experienced in real time through analyzing the music (either aurally or in notation) in order to play even the simplest of pieces. As students progress, they may discover, as I did, that the harmonic overtones they use to tune

"How sour sweet music is when time is broke, and no proportion kept."
— **William Shakespeare**

their instrument relate to the wave theory they are learning in physics class, or that the harmonic structure of the piece they are playing is an expression of the Golden Mean or the Fibonacci Sequence. Whether or not music students learn these particular skills from music is of less importance than creating an opportunity to expand their curiosity for math and science by exploring these connections.

Cultural and Historical Understanding

Music should not be taught in a vacuum. From the very first lesson, the teacher can engage the student in learning music that relates to his world and seeks to broaden his horizons. For example, at our music school, we make a point of using folk songs and masterworks to teach beginners. Learning folk songs from around the world in the early years of study gives children the opportunity to also learn about different cultures (including our own!). As the students grow into playing masterworks (and this could be the greatest works of Beethoven, Bach, or The Beatles), they must learn the history, geography, and culture from which those works came in order to effectively express the message that music conveys. In short, music is an ideal way to engage with and connect to our world.

Appreciation for Art

Something I hear frequently at my Loving Practice, Developing Discipline workshops* is that parents want their children to grow up with an appreciation for great music. For many people, great art speaks powerfully to them on its own (which is what makes it great), but that isn't the case for everyone, especially children. For almost anybody, however, participating in the creation of art sparks appreciation: Either it helps them come to appreciate something, or it deepens their appreciation. I remember how bored I was by symphonies and art galleries as a child before I learned a little painting and a lot of music. Simply recognizing the immense challenge of performing a fast

---

*After offering these at Orpheus Academy of Music for a while, I began to be asked to give them elsewhere, and over the past several years have given these workshops around the country.

trill effortlessly makes hearing that in a concert a source of delight. Being able to understand the harmonic language and the relationship of the melody and rhythms to the text and then to place all of that in a historical context creates what one of my adult students described as a "multi-dimensional experience of immense richness."

Connection to Family

When I interviewed parents whose children studied music and continue to play as adults, over and over again, the number one source of joy these parents described was their kids gladly taking out their instruments when they come home for the holidays. While some families are experiencing increased isolation as each member retreats to her own device, others are coming together in song or simply enjoying music, both live and recorded.

Another way that music can powerfully connect children to their families is through cultural heritage. I ask every student I teach to find out what songs their parents and grandparents loved as children, so I can work those into our lessons. This experience inevitably leads to a level of connection that cannot be replicated any other way. One student I had many years ago was the oldest in a family of five. She was exceptionally responsible with her practice, but rarely showed any joy or even interest in the music I assigned. Then one day, she shared that in a few months they would be going away for a family reunion, and this gave me an idea. I asked her to call her favorite aunt and interview her about her favorite songs. She then chose "Gonna Lay Down My Sword and Shield" to arrange for solo guitar and as a trio to include her two younger sisters, who were taking violin and cello lessons. During the next few months of lessons, she learned about harmony, arranging, overcoming technical challenges, and much more — but most importantly, she did all this with a kind of zeal and joy that made teaching her delightful. When they returned from the reunion, she reported how proud they felt performing that piece and other solos they had prepared.

Self-Esteem

Self-esteem does not come from praise or outside recognition. It comes from the ability to perform a challenging task well at objective levels of excellence. In short, it is being a person that you yourself would esteem. Knowing you have worked long and hard to achieve the skill to do something well is one of the greatest feelings anyone can have. I am no believer in the self-esteem movement — in which every child is rewarded equally for mediocre work — but there is now substantial evidence that self-esteem resulting from objective excellence is one of the most important indicators of future success. Children who believe they are capable of greatness in one area are more likely to believe that they can achieve great things in other areas, to take on greater challenges, and to therefore gain additional skills of which they can be justifiably proud. It is a positive learning cycle that all parents wish for their children.

I would caution, however, that over-emphasis on self-esteem without the virtues of love and humility can easily give rise to an inflated ego, hyper-competitiveness, and self-judgment. The ideal attitude for any musician is humility before the awesomeness of artistic expression, which transcends our personal ego. It is good to recognize how much work your child put into their music, but it's just as important to encourage in them a love of the music. Many students who have become overly concerned with being the best at their instrument are devastated when they hear someone whom they perceive as "better." Ideally, they would find excellence in others inspiring and motivating, not threatening. Maintaining this balance is a challenge in my own family, where my daughter is highly driven and very attracted to competition. Our intention (though I know I often fall short) is to ask her what she loves about each piece and to share our own love of music, from Queen to Stravinsky. This, at least, sends a message that we are interested in beauty, not perfection.

The Development of Life Skills

Of all the many benefits of music study (and what I have listed above certainly only scratches the surface), I believe none so great as the journey of self-discovery that I refer to as *personalized discipline*. Music can be an ideal stone upon which to sharpen our will and our drive to develop curiosity, problem-solving skills, dedication, perseverance, and the habit of deliberate practice, which are all critical to mastering any skill. The focus of this book is how we as parents can provide the framework for developing all this in music lessons and then teach our children to transfer these skills to other areas of their lives.

"Good Enough" Parenting and Teaching

The idea of "Good Enough Parenting" has gained ground as of late. It might seem like an excuse for settling for less rather than reaching for one's highest potential, but, on the contrary, it may actually give our children their best chance to grow into happy, successful people. Essentially, "Good Enough Parenting" (and I would like to extend this idea to "Good Enough Teaching") simply acknowledges the reality that we are human beings — with all the love, beauty, good intentions, and, yes, flaws that that entails. "Good Enough Parenting" gives us permission to admit we don't always know the answers, own up to our shortcomings, and reserve the right to make decisions based on what is good for our unique family. "Good Enough Parenting" isn't settling; it is rebelling against the creativity-killing and energy-sucking pitfalls of the modern expectations on parents that I call "Super-Parenting."

All too frequently, I find myself counseling overwrought parents who are trying to have two successful careers, send their child to a specialized "super school" of some kind, help their child become fluent

> "Good Enough Parenting" simply relieves the pressure of being perfect. You give your child the best chance for success in life by doing your best when you can, apologizing when you fall short, and moving on.

in two or three languages, learn two instruments, be a star soccer player, get straight A's, and engage in making the world a better place. Not surprisingly, their family is stressed out and exhausted most of the time, and practice is just another source of conflict in the home.

I am acutely aware that this book, which attempts to teach the challenging skill of developing discipline, runs the risk of adding yet another task to the "Super-Parent's" already overwhelming life.

However, what I intend to convey are many creative solutions to building a happy, balanced, and disciplined life. Among these solutions, you may find one or several that make your life easier, your struggles with your child less intense, and their progress more enjoyable.

In her book *All Joy and No Fun*, Jennifer Senior discusses the dilemma of the modern parent, which I find beautifully summarized in this meme I saw on Facebook recently:

How To Be A Mom in 2017: *Make sure your children's academic, emotional, psychological, mental, spiritual, physical, nutritional, and social needs are met while being careful not to overstimulate, understimulate Practice, Developing, improperly medicate, helicopter, or neglect them in a screen-free, processed foods–free, GMO-free, negative energy–free, plastic-free, body positive, socially conscious, egalitarian but also authoritative, nurturing but fostering of independence, gentle but not overly permissive, pesticide-free two-story, multilingual home preferably in a cul-de-sac with a backyard and 1.5 siblings spaced at least two years apart for proper development, also don't forget the coconut oil.*

How To Be A Mom In Literally Every Generation Before Ours: *Feed them sometimes.*

(This is why we're crazy.)

— Laditan

I see the struggles of "Super-Parenting" playing out in my own life when, for example, my daughter struggles because I completely forget the schedule and am not able to get a healthy meal prepared before rehearsal. Other times, I may take my frustrations with myself out on her, disrupting her practice as a result.

Not long ago, I was upset at myself for procrastinating all day, and I was staring at the computer screen trying to get started writing, but nothing was coming. Mei Yin was practicing piano in the other room, and I could hear her playing full-speed through a difficult passage of Tchaikovsky: making a mistake, fixing it, and going on; making another mistake, fixing it, and going on. In my head, I told myself that these were mistakes she had been making over and over again for weeks and if she continued this kind of practice, she would permanently learn the passage insecurely, and it would never be right. In a huff, I went and told her as much. A dark look came over her face, and she began playing the passage slowly — but pounding out each note with what sounded like venomous hatred. I returned to my room, took a breath, and considered that I hadn't been at my best when offering my advice, and the results were likewise less than ideal. I went back, apologized, and told her I was just frustrated with how my book was progressing. She asked if I had always practiced carefully as a kid, and I said I never practiced carefully when I was her age — which was why I had to completely relearn how to play guitar when I got to college.

"Good Enough Parenting" is simply a way of relieving the pressure of being perfect. You won't be anyway, so recognize that you give your child the best chance for success in life by doing your best when you can, apologizing when you fall short of your goals, and moving on. We need to be "good enough" parents to provide an environment in which our child is safe, can learn and grow, and have room to make mistakes of their own.

By extension, "Good Enough Teaching" acknowledges that there is no perfect teacher, no perfect lesson, and no perfect curriculum. From time to time at my school, we get parents who bounce from teacher to teacher. At first, they are thrilled with their teacher and the progress of their child, but soon they decide this teacher isn't developing their child's creative side as much as the teacher of their friend's kid. But after a while, they say that the new teacher isn't setting the bar high enough, their child needs more challenges, and they want to switch to that teacher who has students in competitions. Finally, they wonder why their child just "isn't clicking" with any teacher and if maybe they should try another school.

I am concerned that parents will view such a position as suggesting that they should stick with their teacher (namely, me) no matter what. Far from it. I readily admit that I am not the right teacher for all kids; although I do my best to adapt to each child's learning style, there is an intensity and passion to my teaching that doesn't work well with some kids or parents. The same thing is true for all teachers. And unlike family, you can choose your teacher, and you absolutely should do your best to find a good fit.

Finding a "good fit" and finding the "perfect teacher," however, are not the same thing. The former exists (at least in most communities in the U.S.), while the latter does not. Furthermore, optimal learning is a collaboration between the teacher, the parent, and the student — the so-called "Magic Triangle" of education. Hopping from teacher to teacher when things are not going exactly as you had hoped merely masks problems in the communication process, in the commitment to joyful and effective practice at home, or in any number of things. Finally, as valuable as switching to a better fit may be, we must consider that frequent switching halts progress toward building trust, establishing a routine for learning, and allowing the teacher to ascertain a child's learning style.

Remember: our goal is to provide a foundation from which our children can grow in whichever way they choose. Eventually, it will be up to them to choose what they can in their lives while other things will be beyond their control, so we should set a good example by modeling acceptance of ourselves. Teaching them to work and learn within "good enough" situations is a good start.

How to Use This Book

This book describes a process of using music to become a happier and more successful person through joyful and disciplined behavior. However, it is also a practical guide to solving the day-to-day challenges faced by parents trying to get their children to practice. As such, feel free to jump to whichever section best meets your needs at any given time.

However you choose to use this book, know that simply being willing to try different approaches and deliberately creating a positive learning environment at home puts you way ahead of the game. The vast majority of parents, while meaning well, sign up for piano lessons, hope things go well, and if they don't, assume that music just wasn't their child's "thing."

Setting out on a journey to find a better way for your child to embrace music — including all that's involved in gaining and developing the ability to play — does not mean more work or struggle

> If you remember one thing from this book, let it be this motto: "We're sticking with this, and together we'll find a creative way to make it fun."

for you and your family. In fact, it is my hope that it will save you endless hours of reminding, nagging, and power struggles. If you remember one thing from this book, let it be this: *We're sticking with this, and together we will find a creative way to make it fun.* With that, you can allow yourself the time and space to be creative, make mistakes, apologize to each other, learn, and move forward.

I wish you a happy musical journey!

2

REDEFINING DISCIPLINE

Recent research in the areas of learning and skill development overwhelmingly show that we humans are capable of dramatically improving our abilities and our potential. Older ways of thinking presumed that one's intelligence and talent were the predominant factors in determining one's success in a field. Now most parents believe that effective educational experiences can help their child maximize his potential and be successful in whatever area he chooses. What few people understand, however, is that the focused and deliberate application of expert-designed learning strategies over a long period of time can actually *alter the physiological structures of our body and brain so as to dramatically raise our potential.*

Discipline is repeatedly engaging in behaviors that create positive change in our lives. It is the tool that allows for the development of exceptional abilities.

The word *discipline* has a mix of definitions in our culture today. At best it usually refers to the ability to do the things we need to do to accomplish our goals and improve our lives. At worst it brings up images of punishment, as in, "The students were disciplined for their bad behavior." Over the years of conducting Loving Practice, Developing Discipline seminars, I have heard many variations on these two themes, with parents sharing things like:

- "Discipline is being forced to do something you don't want to do."
- "Discipline is doing something you hate so that you can enjoy something you love later."
- "Discipline just isn't for me or my family. We simply don't have it in us."

That last comment (an actual statement from a parent explaining why they couldn't be a part of our music school) points to one of the underlying problems with the concept of discipline in our society today. It is often seen as something you either have or don't have — a trait fixed at birth, given to some and not to others. The research on people who are high achievers through tremendous effort, however, points in a very different direction. According to Anders Ericsson, author of *Peak*, people who exhibit disciplined behavior in one field don't all possess the same defining characteristic that makes them more "effortful" or harder workers than the rest of us. In fact, they don't even demonstrate focused, disciplined behaviors in all areas of their lives.

People who are highly disciplined in an area typically use a wide variety of strategies to motivate themselves to work hard and achieve their goals. For one student, the desire to connect with family and play the music she loves was highest on the list. For another, performing in talent shows, recitals, and later competitions made the biggest difference. For both, having a written practice schedule, clearly attainable goals, and recognition for their efforts was important to their success. The point is that discipline is not a trait, but a suite of strategies that are effective for maintaining positive change over a long period of time. Furthermore, these focus strategies are clearly something that can be taught and learned — something that can make a significant difference even if we only pick up a few new skills each year and, because the journey of learning our own motivations is never ending, that we can improve upon for a lifetime.

I like to define discipline as all the little things we do that make our motivation strong enough to overcome the inherent challenges of meaningful change. Discipline is a process of self-discovery — gradually learning how we can motivate ourselves to do those things we know will bring us one step closer to our most important goals.

With this definition of discipline as a group of healthy skills put toward a singular focus, hundreds of little behaviors that we may not have thought very important by themselves take on new meaning.

- *Discipline is getting enough sleep.*
  A survey of violinists at a conservatory found that the top players (those who went on to solo careers) actually got as many as five hours more sleep per week than mid-tier players.

- *Discipline is staying inspired.*
  Frequently the top performers in a field credit their idols and their peers for inspiring them to keep going and reach for a higher result. In music, inspiration can come from buying the latest album of your favorite artist, looking up songs online, or going to concerts.

- *Discipline is knowing how to make difficult activities fun.*
  I remember my daughter thought up a game when she was just five where she would line up her stuffed animals, then play her pieces on guitar while I improvised a little dance. When she was done playing, she would make each animal give its American Idol™–style score of my dancing.

- *Discipline is signing up for a deadline.*
  Every music teacher will tell you her students make more progress the weeks before the studio recital than the rest of the year put together. Among my musician friends, I would estimate less than one in ten practices beyond a very minimal amount unless they are preparing for a concert. From the perspective of our non-musical friends, it often seems as though we practice for months and then give a concert or go on tour, when, in fact it is the opposite. We schedule a concert a few months in the future that we are completely unprepared to play and then begin to practice in earnest, mostly to save ourselves from the public embarrassment of performing badly or canceling.

Discipline Is Like Building a Fire

When we're learning a new skill, cultivating the desire to practice can be like trying to start a fire with wood that is too damp. With music, we want to feel the warmth of expression and the comfort of knowing we can play anything we set our minds to, but everything feels like a struggle. As parents, we can feel like we are trying to light a fire inside our child, but it keeps sputtering and going out.

Allow me to take this analogy a little further: When we light a real fire, we build it with paper and kindling. We give it plenty of room for air and good fuel to grow. We don't throw a big heavy log on a young fire before it is ready. Once the flames are going strong, we can relax and just keep feeding it from time to time, enjoying the warmth. However, if the fire burns down again, we will need to return to the rebuilding process with care.

The initial period of learning must be approached thoughtfully and with great skill. This is why Sophia Gilmson, head of the piano pedagogy program at The University of Texas at Austin, is fond of saying, "If I could make one rule, it would be this: Only the best teachers are allowed to teach beginners!" It takes great expertise to stoke the passion and build the skills needed for great art in a young child. Great music, appropriate techniques, gradually increasing performance opportunities, sincere praise, clear direction and feedback on how to improve — these things are the dry wood and kindling with which the fire is built. I believe the spark for creativity exists in every child; we simply need to prepare the fuel.

Discipline Is Like Saving for Retirement

Okay, so this might not be the easiest analogy for kids to relate to (and perhaps many adults), but I recently heard the Nobel Prize–winning behavioral economist Richard Thaler say something that sounded exactly like the way I explain discipline to parents:

> Figuring out how much to save for retirement is a really hard cognitive problem that very few economists have solved for themselves. And it's not only cognitively hard, it involves delay of gratification, which people find hard.... When I was first working with ... the first "Nudge unit," the phrase I kept saying in every meeting ... was, "If you want to get people to do something, make it easy. Remove the barriers." That's what we're about.

If we think of practicing music (or anything for that matter) as building up a savings account of skills, then the process of becoming wealthy in "talent" is one of putting off the activities with immediate gratification (eating ice cream, watching TV, etc.) and instead choosing to do the hard things. If we want our children to fill up their personal skills account with things that will make them successful, happy, and contributing members of society, we need to make it as easy as possible for them to engage in the behaviors that will grow those skills.

Thaler was, in part, responsible for popularizing the use of the 401(K) auto-enroll as a means of getting a larger portion of the population to save for retirement. Particularly, he espoused the idea of "auto-escalation," in which workers agree to a manageable savings amount to start, but then sign up to increase the amount they are contributing each year by a single percentage. In other words, if you asked a new employee to immediately begin setting aside 10 percent of his paycheck on the first day, he would likely balk. If you ask him, however, to set aside 3 percent and automatically increase the amount he was saving by 1 percent a year until he reached 15 percent, he is much more likely to agree.

Similarly, if we ask our children to practice an amount of time each day equal to the length of their lesson, they might be unprepared for such an undertaking (particularly if they start with thirty-minute lessons at age four, as is quite common). If we ask them, however, to practice five minutes per day, and increase the amount they practice by five minutes each week until they reach 20, 30, or 40 minutes (depending on their age), we are not only likely to get agreement, but they will end up practicing more.

Unfortunately, practicing is not as straightforward as programming a payroll system somewhere to take an additional percentage out. We, as parents, need to keep track of the practice time each day. Furthermore, there are other "barriers" that get in the way of practice (broken instruments, birthday parties, too much homework, etc.). Nevertheless, we can take the same basic approach: Make it easy for them to make the most beneficial decision.

One of the moments I am most proud of as a father was when my daughter, in an exhausted voice, came to me and said, "I just don't feel like practicing; I need some motivation." With this sentence, we were able to embark upon a discussion that led not only to her being willing to practice that day, but has also helped her approach dreaded chores or homework she doesn't want to do. The activities she has noticed help motivate her at this age are things like listening to her favorite artists on YouTube, beginning her practice by reviewing old favorites, and deciding to go for a bike ride down to the park after she practices. The important thing is that she is asking the question, "How can I motivate myself today?" because that is the question she will need to ask herself over and over when she faces difficult tasks in life.

So, the next time you wonder if you or your child are disciplined enough to achieve your goals, try reframing the question: "What can I do right now that will make taking the next step possible, or even fun?" Because discipline is a process of learning what little things work for us, gradually building upon those, and making a conscious choice to fill our lives with those behaviors.

Too often what I see from parents is an attempt to get their child to practice in a way that worked for them as children, or worked for their teachers, or they see working for another child (either an older sibling or a friend), without the recognition that each of us needs to find what works for us personally. More importantly, when we engage our children in ever-evolving conversations about what is working for them to motivate themselves to do the challenging work of self-improvement, we are building the foundation for their own self-reflective ability to analyze their goals, understand their motivations, and act to bring those goals to fruition. In short, we give them the tools for a successful life.

Personalized Discipline

"You have to know your child, then help them to know themselves."
– **JAY, SARAH'S DAD**

If discipline is simply engaging in behaviors that improve our life, then why don't we all simply copy the behaviors of people who are successful and leave it at that? In fact, a whole industry of self-help books approach discipline in essentially this manner: They describe successful people in the glowing details of their perfection (usually leaving out their character flaws) and then encourage us to emulate them. Tom Brady's exceptional tolerance for pain and willingness to get back up after each punishing hit and work harder than anyone else; Andrés Segovia's insistence that he practiced five hours every day, at least two of those hours on scales; Bobby Fischer reading chess strategy books during school rather than paying attention in class.

Too often we try to engage in disciplined behaviors that we have seen in famous musicians, athletes, or scholars without asking why that behavior worked for them and if it is a good fit for us. Worse, many people observe a few examples of disciplined behavior, realize that their situation makes that kind of behavior impossible, and then use that as an excuse for why they cannot be successful. It isn't that we shouldn't draw inspiration from the success of others – quite the opposite! Reading about Segovia's two-hour scale practice motivated me to practice scales as much as I could in high school (topping out at about 30 minutes). Still, I have my doubts now that, without clear guidance about *why* I should practice those scales, it yielded any significant improvement to my guitar playing.

One of the characteristics shared by hundreds of parents of successful music students whom I have known and interviewed for this book is the insistence that you have to know your child and tailor your approach to each child. For example, Alan Johnston noticed that his middle child was motivated by pizza and therefore made a game where repeating a phrase many times earned "pizza slices" that could be turned in for a pizza night. His youngest, however, hated multiple repetitions, so he challenged that son to perfectly master a phrase in just a few tries with his eyes closed (which he did). Another parent told me that because both of his kids were relatively motivated to practice music for its own sake, his role was usually to make sure they had the time set aside and then notice when they needed either a little more focus or needed to let go of their perfectionism and take a break.

Conversely, most of the power struggles I have witnessed were the result of parents who felt their child had to conform to a "best" way of practicing without noticing how their individual child learned best (I myself have often been guilty of this mistake). One of the hazards of reading hundreds of books, papers, and interviews on effective practice strategies is that it has become difficult to listen to my daughter struggling and not want to jump in and offer practice advice, even when she is in the midst of finding her own way.

Another common mistake that I believe is exacerbated by research into excellence is the tendency to try to emulate "the average peak performer." We read that top performers practiced an average of 10,000 hours, had two supportive parents, a top-notch coach, overcame a personal struggle, got 8.7 hours of sleep a night, and won their first competition at age eight and a half. What we miss in all of this data is that *none* of the top performers matched every characteristic of the average top performers. Some were orphans, some got very little sleep or practice, or had no teacher. It isn't that these things don't matter; it's just that it is more important to notice what works to motivate *your* child.

I am reminded of an analogy I once read (I can't remember where) used by a Zen master to teach his disciples to accept their own unique personality. We are each born with a spirit that is like a horse we ride throughout life. Some horses are swift, some slow and steady, some easy to train, and some stubborn. Too often we waste time wishing that we had been born with a different personality than we have — one that is swift, sure-footed, and easily follows our commands. If we learn to ride the horse we are on, we not only increase our chances of getting somewhere, but we may even enjoy the ride! In other words, it is not the horse, but the rider with whom we should be concerned. Our mission in life is to learn how to best work with our own personality.

One aspect of disciplined behavior that struck me early on in my studies with many great musicians was that, although all of them worked hard toward getting better, their motivations and practice habits varied dramatically. To be sure, there was some overlap, but for the most part, each disciplined person had his own way of staying motivated. Some enjoyed practicing at night, others first thing in the morning. Some would dive right into their hardest pieces, and others believed firmly in a thorough technical warmup. Some had entered many competitions when young, and others avoided them altogether. The list could go on and on. What I found curious was how often some of them would describe their own path as the "right way" that should be followed to success by all – yet so many other masters were successful doing something completely different!

Personalized discipline is an approach to engaging in disciplined behaviors in a way that fits well with our own unique personality and lifestyle. It is a constant journey of testing what works for us, discarding what is not working, and refining what is. At its core, it is a journey of self-discovery that, when applied to all areas of life, allows us to experience growth joyfully — even when (or maybe especially when) that growth is challenging.

Helping your child become a disciplined person who understands how to motivate herself will provide her with the confidence she needs to accomplish challenging goals, learn new skills, and even build her own character to enhance the qualities that will be most helpful to her.

In becoming disciplined, we learn that all desirable change is difficult by nature, but that we are confident in our ability to accomplish difficult things. We experience firsthand that building new neural structures, like building muscle, requires effortfully breaking things down and rebuilding them into new and stronger patterns. That is why we focus on understanding our own unique personality and then building an effective set of motivations that work for us. Once we know how to push our own buttons, we can activate ourselves to engage in the behaviors that create real change.

The Difficulty of Change and the Power of Discipline

Understanding discipline as the act of creating positive change in our lives, whether through building new skills, muscles, thinking patterns, or anything else, doesn't change the fact that meaningful change is always exceptionally difficult. It simply means that there is a way to foster the grit to develop amazing abilities. As I like to say to my students when they complain that playing guitar is so difficult, "If this were easy, nobody would be impressed that you can do it so well!"

We can see that the very thing that makes disciplined behavior valuable (namely, the significant change created within us) is the thing that will make it difficult. Building new neural structures, new muscles, new habits, etc., is hard work. It is hard work even for mature adults who may have a strong motivation and the time and resources to enact that change. How often have you seen friends (or perhaps yourself) unable or unwilling to make meaningful changes in their lives even though the consequences for continuing on their current path will clearly be ruinous to their health, finances, or relationships?

This is because change is hard for everyone. For children — whose brains have not yet developed significant impulse control or long attention spans and who have not yet experienced the rewards of self-improvement (just to name a few strikes against them) — engaging in disciplined behavior can feel like torture. *In fact, it is torture if we don't build that discipline upon a foundation of love and self-awareness.*

This is, essentially, the reason I decided to write this book. Through the study of music (among other things), teachers, students, and artists have found and shared ways to build their motivation and overcome the obstacles to their practice to a degree that I believe may be unique in human endeavors. I will share with you the practice tips and motivational tricks that musicians (and others) have shared with me through lessons, conversation, books, articles, workshops, and anywhere else I could find them. Most of my life has been spent in pursuit of learning and practicing disciplined behaviors. From the time I first picked up a guitar and realized that my clumsy fingers couldn't make the sounds I heard others around me performing so

> For children, disciplined behavior can feel like torture. It *is* torture if we don't build that discipline upon a foundation of love and self-awareness.

effortlessly, I have been on this journey to discover how I can make the most significant improvements in the shortest amount of time and enjoy doing it. I consider myself eminently fortunate to have chosen music as the path for my life because I believe this path has given me the tools for a successful and happy life. My greatest honor is to share those skills with my daughter, my students, and the world.

Music and the Development of Discipline

Music study provides a wonderful vehicle for this journey of self-discovery. Adam Holzman, international concert artist, and my own teacher, says his parents signed all three of their children up for music lessons to teach them discipline, never expecting that that would yield not one but two professional musicians. In truth, any challenging activity that interests you may be your medium for practicing discipline, but I think there are several aspects of music study that make it particularly effective for this purpose.

- **Music is inherently attractive** on many levels to people of all ages. Most people, especially children, are immediately drawn to a lovely melody or exciting rhythm and experience a powerful desire to be able to make music themselves. Nurturing this motivation is the key to building a willingness to do hard things.
- **It is easy to get started.** With a good teacher, we can experience success playing a simple melody on most instruments within minutes of beginning our first lesson.
- **Music can be sequenced to gradually increase difficulty.** Good music teachers have studied how to sequence the challenges encountered in music study so that the student grows *gradually* into taking on unbelievably complex and beautiful pieces of music, allowing students to stay engaged for a lifetime of practice.
- **Music study has a tradition of daily individual home practice.** While many other challenging activities that promote discipline (martial arts, sports, chess, etc.) often provide group settings in which practice takes place, it is generally expected that you will practice music alone much of the time. This requires the development of self-discipline in a way other fields don't always foster (though, to be sure, the greatest in any field practiced independently).
- **Music provides regular opportunities to achieve meaningful goals** that can be highly motivating, namely, concerts. From performing for our teacher in the lesson, to playing for family, to recitals, band concerts, and in professional settings, music has a built-in intrinsic reward system that can be satisfying and even exhilarating.
- **Music has ever-expanding challenges** in the physical, intel-lectual, and emotional realms. The coordination involved in playing a simple scale is multiplied millions of times over as the student musician grows into the ability to easily perform a twenty-minute concerto by memory. The understanding that

music is made of sounds moving up and down in pitch with different timings grows as they understand notation, music theory, and eventually musical analysis and historically appropriate stylistic interpretation. Finally, all the technical and musical perfection in the world is meaningless if the student does not become an artist who can apply her own personal expression to the music.

Ishaan's Story

Let me illustrate how discipline can grow through the story of one of my current students.

Several summers ago, a family came to my music school with a four-year-old child named Ishaan. I told them that this was a little younger than I generally recommended starting lessons, but I would be happy to show him how to play a little tune on the guitar, tell them about our approach to learning, and learn about their goals for Ishaan. During the ten minutes it took for him to learn "Conga Line" (that catchy tune often played at Hawaiian-themed parties, when doing the "limbo"), I observed that he had an intense fascination with the guitar and a sufficient attention span and the coordination to make playing guitar possible without it being prohibitively difficult. I discussed with the parents that beginning at this age would require that they learn along with Ishaan and practice with him every day at home. They were, naturally, concerned that they might not be able to learn guitar or to make practice at home enjoyable or even successful. I assured them that I had already taught hundreds of other

Ishaan at his Home Concert
Photo courtesy of Shruti Jha

families how to learn, how to play, and how to make it fun. Perhaps it was Ishaan's eagerness to learn, his parents' trust in him or me, or something else entirely, but they made the very significant first step of signing up and committing themselves fully.

Over the past three years, Ishaan has learned over 100 folk songs as well as popular and classical melodies, through which he mastered the basic techniques of the guitar, came to understand the underpinnings of melody and rhythm, and deepened his love of music. He has shown particular interest in improvisation and composition, so whenever we get a new concept, I play improvisation games with him, and he often comes back to the lesson with a new composition he has created. At the end of the second year, he performed a "Home Concert" for his friends, neighbors, and family (even some from halfway across the country). His focus through the concert and his delight when it was over was something I will always cherish witnessing. His parents reported that he wouldn't set his guitar down for the entire weekend after that concert. The following year, he made a CD of his favorite songs, and the year after that, he traveled with a number of students from our school to perform at Carnegie Hall in New York City, both solo and as part of a large ensemble. For each of these goals, he had to stretch his abilities both physically and mentally, often undertaking practicing twice a day for a period of months leading up to the goal. Along the way he has used his recitals to raise money for supporting food pantries at low-income schools in Austin and education programs for kids in rural India. He has also raised funds to support an organization called HeartGift that provides life-saving heart surgeries to underprivileged kids around the world with congenital heart defects, much like the surgery he himself received when he was an infant to mend the hole in his heart. He performs regularly at his school, especially when he can play a piece of music that exemplifies the topic being taught, such as when he played and sang "Los Pollitos" in Spanish class.

Ishaan's abilities now at age seven are those of an exceptional and well-rounded musician: He has solid technical ability and can learn many pieces in many styles; he has solid musical abilities and can learn by ear, read music, improvise, and come up with lovely compositions on the spot. He is by no means a musical prodigy, but I have no doubt that if he maintains his current level of progress that he will achieve the level of mastery associated with concert musicians sometime in his late teens or early twenties. This doesn't mean that I will be disappointed if he doesn't become a professional concert musician; it simply means that he will have the ability to express himself at that level of artistry. Furthermore (and more importantly, in my opinion), he will have learned the disciplined behaviors that lead to the highest levels of expertise, which will therefore allow him to achieve the same level of success at anything to which he sets his mind.

Without a doubt, Ishaan started with an exceptional interest in music that continues to this day (when I play music for him in the lesson, his eyes go wide with wonder, and he often makes the most astounding observations about the beauty of music). Nevertheless, in most respects, he is a regular boy like any other I have taught: He is often distracted, tired, and unfocused in the lesson. If given the chance, he will talk, without pause, for the entire lesson. His parents both work, so he doesn't get home until after 6:00 PM each day and must do homework, eat, play, and get to bed in a few short hours, leaving little time for practice. Given the choice, he would rather improvise for hours or play pieces he is already good at than work on difficult sections or techniques that require him to improve his skills.

So how has Ishaan developed such an exceptional level of skill and the willingness to engage in intense practice for extended periods of time each day when so many other children find it a struggle just to learn "Twinkle, Twinkle Little Star?" The answer to his success is a summary of everything that I will present in this book:

- He began by falling in love with music and nurturing that love throughout his journey. My impression is that his parents, who love music, had begun this process when he was an infant.
- His parents established a regular but manageable practice schedule (10–15 minutes a day to start, growing gradually over the years).
- His parents were willing to try many different approaches to making practice for a four-year-old fun until they settled into what worked for them.
- He learned solid technical, musical, and practice habits from an early age so his learning would not be impeded.
- He made musical friends at his music school and his regular

school with whom he could play, so music was a social as well as personal experience.

- He was able to associate music with his life in ways that were meaningful and powerful.
- He experienced numerous rewarding performance experiences in which his hard work was rewarded by the experience of playing at the top of his abilities and having a large audience appreciate his music.
- His entire family, including grandparents, aunts, uncles, and cousins, support his music study and genuinely appreciate what a powerful gift he has.

It is easy to look at highly successful people in any field and assume that they have some hidden talent or special character trait that we do not have. The research, however, seems to point in a different direction: Exceptionally "talented" people, whether they be musicians, athletes, or scientists, are more likely to share a sequence of experiences than a character trait. Experiences that support and stoke their passion, teach them to be disciplined, help them master expert practice techniques, and experience the success of their efforts are much more important than any physical or intellectual predisposition.

Talent is not merely a genetic predisposition, but a heightened rate of learning due to neural and physical advantages — advantages you have the power to gain. Since disciplined practice over time improves the structure of the brain, when you engage in it, you aren't just "reaching your potential" — you are *increasing* your potential. So while Child A might have some neural advantages over Child B at age one, by the age of seven, as the result of environment, experience, and effort, Child B might have rearranged her neural network to be more sensitive to musical sounds and have a vastly superior musical mind to Child A. Therefore, at this point, we would have to say seven-year-old Child B is "more talented."

What this means is that a joyful and successful pursuit of excellence is within the purview of all who wish to follow a path of discipline. Furthermore, truly effective discipline is not a painful litany of unpleasant tasks, but the creative process of finding what works for us and sticking with it over a long period of time. In short, it is a process that can bring happiness and success to our lives in all areas.

3

THE THREE PILLARS OF EFFECTIVE CHANGE

When we are disciplined over a long period of time, it gives us the chance to develop habits of learning and behavior that we can transfer to new areas of learning. The process of effective learning and skill development involves three key areas for maximum improvement:

- **Learner's Mindset**
- **Grit**
- **Deliberate Practice**

Having a *learner's mindset* allows us to engage in learning with curiosity and a willingness to face challenges without fear of failure because we realize that failure is simply part of the learning process.

Grit is the ability to stick with challenges long enough to make meaningful, lasting change.

Deliberate practice is a set of practice strategies that lead to maximum improvement in the shortest amount of time.

Three Pillars of Effective Change

A Learner's Mindset	Grit	Deliberate Practice
Learning with curiosity	Stick with challenges long enough to improve	Strategies that lead to maximum improvement in a short time
No fear of judgement		

When all three of these are present, we are not only able to achieve phenomenal results, we can also enjoy the process of getting there. Not only can we change our potential, we can also learn to think of ourselves as capable of adapting to meet any challenge.

I wish I could say that simply practicing music for ten years will inevitably lead to the development of these powerful skills for learning. Unfortunately, observing thousands of students over the years in my own private guitar lessons and at my music school has taught me that, in the vast majority of cases, students will not learn these vital skills through luck alone. Just as you can't expect to learn a difficult piece of music without a plan to master its challenges, you cannot expect a child to develop complex skills without a teacher who excels in teaching those skills and a parent who supports that learning. It *is* possible that they will happen upon some of those skills if they are highly motivated, but as the saying goes, "Hope is not a strategy for success."

Typically, without guidance from an experienced teacher, parents fall into one of two categories when approaching music lessons: They either force their children to practice every day, or they leave it entirely up to the child. If children are forced to practice without developing their own love of music and their own plan for success, they will usually quit music as soon as allowed, and they will certainly not have had the opportunity to learn the lessons of self-discipline. Conversely, when I observe children whose parents say it is up to the child to pursue music on their own (in essence, expecting them to learn these skills entirely without guidance), what I generally see is a very low level of accomplishment followed by dropping out and, again, nothing of value that can be transferred to other areas of their lives.

When teachers and parents collaborate to form an environment where curiosity is nurtured, tools for learning and achieving goals are taught, and a firm commitment to seeing goals through is maintained, then children experience a high level of success and, over time, develop life skills that lead to successful outcomes.

Far beyond "successful outcomes," there is something almost indescribable that always occurs when children develop musically in an environment that nurtures these traits. In the course of finding what is interesting and meaningful to the child and celebrating it in our lives, there will be moments of pure magic that take our breath away, if we are alert to them. It may be as subtle as a phrase overheard from another room played with such feeling that it brings a tear to your eye, or a chance to connect with grandparents by learning their favorite childhood songs. For all the developmental benefits of music, we should never lose sight of the fact that the most powerful benefits of music lie in the present moment — the one in which our child is sharing something artistic and meaningful with us.

Learner's Mindset

How effectively our children learn varies dramatically from one environment to another and one moment to another. As a parent and a teacher, I've experienced how disconcerting this can be: The child was getting the concept last week, but now he is struggling and easily frustrated. What changed?

In teaching, we tend to focus on the curricula, our sequencing, our presentation, and so forth, and it is easy to overlook the fact that all learning takes place in the mind of the learner. Unless that mind is ready for learning and prepared to grow, change, and tackle new challenges, nothing we do can make a difference. There are many things that impact whether a child is ready to learn something: from his knowledge base and interest to his emotional or physical state (ever puzzled over your child throwing a tantrum over a minor thing, only to find out he is running a fever?). One essential element that is often overlooked, however, is how children perceive themselves in the learning process.

In her groundbreaking book *Mindset*, Dr. Carol Dweck describes how people can shift from a state of mind focused on curiosity and effort (a "Growth Mindset") to a state of mind focused on fear of being judged as stupid or incompetent (a "Fixed Mindset"). Through her extensive research, she has demonstrated that people are highly sensitive to verbal and social cues, which can easily cause them to move out of the growth mindset, where one naturally and joyfully focuses on learning, to the fixed mindset. In my experience, children who are concerned about what others are thinking about them frequently are completely paralyzed from engaging in music effectively. Perhaps they can fight through spelling or math while feeling judged, but music requires such intense focus that if we are distracted by thoughts of inadequacy, we tend to freeze.

Sadly, many of the accolades we give to children in the hopes of encouraging them actually have the opposite effect, in that they promote the fixed mindset — a state of mind in which children think they are being judged based on how effortlessly they can master a task. This is unfortunate because *effort* is really the primary thing that can actually make them "talented."

A typical study done by Dr. Dweck was one in which first-graders were given a puzzle to solve that was designed for kindergarteners, so something they would likely solve relatively easily. Half the kids in the study were told, "Wow, good job; you're really smart!" when they had finished the puzzle. The other half received no verbal cue. Next, the kids were given a puzzle to solve that was at a second-grade level. The interesting thing is that the children who were told they were "smart" not only had more trouble with the second puzzle, but they were much more likely to give up sooner and make comments such as, "This is stupid," or "I don't like this." The kids who weren't told anything, on the other hand, were much more likely to say such things as, "I like puzzles," and "Can I take this home with me? I want to work on it some more."

Music provides an excellent opportunity to enter into our growth mindset because it is so immediate and requires staying "in the moment" to perform well. So, in the ideal setting, music inherently draws us into a learner's mindset and away from concerns of what others may be thinking about us. Unfortunately, the severe talent bias in our culture (the belief that inherent musical talent, rather than hard work, is the most important trait for learning music) can be detrimental to that learner's mindset.

Students who are in love with music and unaware of the judgment of others engage so fully that they are able to make progress even as they make mistakes. As Dr. Dweck observes, "Not only weren't they discouraged by failure, they didn't even think they were failing. They thought they were learning." Over time, these students naturally surpass those who were originally judged as "talented" but were living in fear of losing that title. It is our responsibility to remind them how hard they worked to develop musical skill because we won't be able to stop their grandparents and other fawning adults from gushing about their exceptional "talent."

34

The best way to help our kids focus on their effort rather than their talent is either to praise specific focused behaviors or, better yet, to simply engage them in conversations about what they like about the music. In the short-term, it can feel right to praise our child's talent; she has just warmed our hearts with the most beautiful song, so naturally we want to shout her talent from the rooftops, to which she will respond with joy and pride! When she inevitably encounters difficulty on the next practice, however, she will remember how proud we were when she played well and naturally think she is failing to reach our expectations. "After the experience with difficulty, the performance of the ability-praised students plummeted, even when we gave them some more of the easier problems.... The effort kids showed better and better performance" (Dweck 71–72).

Unfortunately, this is not something we can solve once and for all. Our kids will get messages that they are being judged on their looks, their race, their gender, their intelligence, and a dozen other fixed traits over which they have no control. We must deliberately engage them in thinking about their growth and effort over their entire lives. As Dr. Dweck says, "It's amazing — once a problem improves, people often *stop doing what caused it to improve.* Once you feel better, you stop taking your medicine" (242–43).

Grit

If we wish to accomplish anything of value, it will require more than simply a curious mind and a passing interest. We will need to be able to stick with something tenaciously for a very long period of time. It will require the resiliency to bounce back from failures and setbacks, the willpower to keep working even when we aren't at our best, and the habit of regular practice in order to make steady improvement.

The researcher Dr. Angela Duckworth has been studying the effects of long-term commitment on goal-oriented self-improvement. Among other places, her research took her to West Point, where she studied and helped the military develop a test that could predict which cadets were most likely to make it through the rigorous training. In the end, her simple "Grit Scale" proved more predictive

> *"Before hard work comes play."*
> —**Angela Duckworth**

of success than anything the Army had come up with before. The top performers at West Point, Dr. Duckworth found, "not only had determination, they had *direction*.... It was this combination of passion and perseverance that made high achievers special."

Furthermore, Duckworth's research shows that grit is something we can build over time. If grit is one of the best predictors for success in difficult endeavors, then it is accordingly one of the highest values we can impart to our children. Music provides us with an ideal medium for practicing gritty behavior. Duckworth describes four steps to a grittier child:

- **Interest**
- **Practice**
- **Connection to something outside ourselves**
- **Hope**

Just as with discipline, we often associate the concept of grit with the willingness to drag ourselves through the mud, underneath barbwire, in the rain, rather than with laughter and joyful play. Joy, however, is where grit begins. As Duckworth says, "Before hard work comes play." We must stoke interest before we can begin to practice, connect to the world outside ourselves, and dream of greatness. It must always go in that order: interest → practice → connection → hope.

Developing Grit through Desirable Difficulty

If we begin by creating interest through joyful play, however, we must eventually encounter challenge and even frustration in order to develop an appetite for sustained hard work. In fact, most of the time, if something remains too easy, most kids will become bored and lose interest. Gradually increasing the level of challenge — where they are operating at the edge of their ability, always growing and improving, and seeing the fruits of their efforts — allows children to stay engaged and develop a strong work ethic.

In my role as academy director, I occasionally find myself feeling like I am talking out of both sides of my mouth. One moment, I am emphasizing the value of developing the grit to take on tough challenges and work diligently toward a solution; other times, I am working with teachers to create the most effortless path toward mastery. How do we reconcile these competing goals of "making it fun" and "desirable difficulty?"

First of all, we must recognize that not all difficulty is desirable and not every kind of fun practice leads to greater enthusiasm or skill. For difficulty to be desirable, it needs to be overcome in a time period and manner that allows learners to reflect on their achievement and thereby build a greater capacity and desire to accomplish worthwhile goals in the future. Giving a four-year-old a piece of music that will require over a year to learn defies everything we know about cognitive development for children that age. Difficulty of this sort is unlikely to lead to greater confidence in one's ability to overcome future challenges.

At the same time, older students must encounter challenges regularly, or they quickly become bored. Many of my more advanced students, including my own daughter, beg to be allowed to play the most difficult pieces because they know playing those pieces is a demonstration that they have achieved great skill, because they can "show off" in concert, and most of all because those pieces are often very complex and interesting. Leveraging this intense desire to play appropriately difficult music is one of the most important tasks facing any teacher. Giving a student a piece that is too difficult simply because they promise to practice diligently can lead to tension and injury, but advancing too slowly will almost certainly lead to boredom and eventually to terminating lessons.

To help myself, and my teachers, understand this concept, I often refer to students as having two bank accounts labeled "Motivation" and "Skill." Building skill requires the expenditure of effort, which will draw upon our motivational reserves.

Ideally, a student arrives at the first lesson brimming with enthusiasm that can be harnessed toward developing the skills necessary for beautiful music-making. An excellent teacher provides a series of musical experiences through which the student may work to develop the ability to play a few easy songs. This will require some effort, which, in turn, may temporarily lower the amount of enthusiasm the student has for playing. We might encounter a few complaints like, "It's too hard!" or "I don't want to practice." If the music is enjoyable, however, and he is able play it well enough to hear that and feel proud of himself for his accomplishment, he will usually experience enough of a boost to his motivation to provide the energy required to master the next skill.

A skillful teacher will sense when it is appropriate to allow the student to struggle with a difficult concept while projecting confidence in the child's ability to overcome the challenge. If small challenges are encountered and overcome regularly, most children will naturally begin seeking out larger challenges on their own, such as downloading sheet music, learning something by ear, or making their own arrangement of a favorite piece of music. Students who have been spoon-fed every step of the way and given all the answers will be unlikely to trust their own abilities and likely to retreat eventually into doing the bare minimum of their assigned work.

Another challenge can occur even when the teacher and parent are adept and careful in all their choices. Occasionally, there may be an unforeseen complication: The teacher has misjudged the difficulty level for this particular piece; the parent has been unduly critical of practice at home due to stressors beyond his control, home practice was impossible for several days, and now the student can't remember how to play what she learned in the lesson; ... or a hundred other possible challenges. I can honestly say that this has happened at some point along the way of every successful student I have ever taught — including those who have gone on to music careers. Ideally, the difficulty is caught early and discussed openly and without shame or blame. The teacher may say, "Hmm. I think there is a better piece that will be more fun for you; we can come back to this one later." Or the parent can come to the lesson and explain, "I'm so sorry, we had family over all weekend, and my child can't remember how to play 'Hot Cross Buns.' Can you help us with that again?"

Deliberate Practice

"Deliberate practice," a term coined by Anders Ericsson in his research on exceptional performers, is the use of specific training techniques that have been developed by experts to increase the efficiency and effectiveness of our practice such that we can maximize our growth. Some fields, such as chess, martial arts, and classical music have traditions dating back hundreds of years that have allowed them to invent, test, and record vast collections of study methods. Others, such as heart surgery, airplane piloting, and certain sports have been the subject of intense study because of the high demand or necessity for extreme levels of excellence. Either way, there is ample evidence that intense study using specialized learning systems can lead to astonishing results.

Deliberate practice makes exceptional skill possible by increasing the speed and efficiency of our learning through specialized practice techniques, but it will still take a long time to reach expert levels. Unfortunately, there is no magic formula to become phenomenally good at a complex skill in a short amount of time. (Of course, if there were, we would simply redefine what it means to be "exceptional" because everyone would be able to do it!) Dr. Ericsson's estimate of 10,000 hours needed to reach world-class excellence is too broad to be applied to every individual, but it is a good idea to remember that developing excellence will require many years of intense daily training. Some skills may require more, some less; some people need more time and some less, but it is safe to say that with all complex skills, it will take a long time (at least five to ten years) of intense study, using specialized practice techniques to reach the highest levels of performance.

Deliberate practice makes possible the neurological and physiological changes in the mind and body necessary for extremely high levels of performance. And here's the rub: *It is the very fact that you are making significant improvement that makes these learning techniques so difficult.* Stopping, moving extremely slowly through the mistake to discover exactly what muscle, what miscue, what confusion, is causing the problem, and then repeating this process until every tiny detail is perfect — this is almost painfully difficult for even the most dedicated professional. Breaking old habits and carefully building up new ones is akin to building muscle. It requires us to push ourselves right up to the breaking point and then to rest and let our brains build up the new structures. No wonder so few are capable of this day in and day out for years!

Casual practice, by contrast, is what parents often refer to as "playing for fun." It is what I do when I run in the morning or play ping-pong. I have no intention of improving my run time or entering ping-pong competitions; I simply enjoy these activities in the moment and forget about them when I am done. To be sure, there is nothing wrong with having things in our lives that we enjoy and make no deliberate attempt to improve in. Perhaps it is even unwise to attempt to "be the best" at everything we do because we have a limited supply of the physical and mental resources necessary for intense focus, and we should reserve that precious energy for the few areas in which we wish to excel rather than trying to be a "Jack of all trades."

In my experience, the difference in speed of improvement between someone using specialized practice techniques and someone simply "playing for fun" is not entirely evident at the beginning stages of study. And this is borne out in the study of other fields. A person who starts

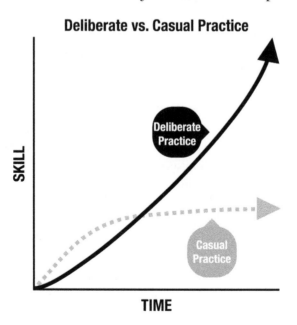

running every day will see significant improvement in their run times and cardiovascular health in the first year; someone who decides to get good at memorizing names (as I did several years ago) can significantly improve simply by trying. This doesn't mean their skill will eventually reach exceptional levels if they "just keep at it." A self-taught guitarist will often be capable of playing more impressive songs after one year than the student who comes to train seriously at an academy. But, the casual practitioner will quickly reach a limit to his skill and even find that that skill declines slightly as he gets bored with his lack of progress, while the deliberate practicer reaches an exceptional level of artistry, which outsiders assume is attributable to "natural talent."

Music (especially classical music) is one of the most studied areas of skill development when it comes to researching advanced practice techniques. There is both a long history of master musicians sharing their practice techniques as well as a great deal of academic research into the most effective ways of learning classical music. For my own part, as a "late" beginner (at age ten), I have always had an intense interest in which practice techniques could yield the fastest results because I wanted to catch up with my peers who had started at younger ages. So, as it happens, across the thousands of sources, from both musicians and research, a few practice strategies have emerged that are consistently recommended for optimal improvement. Among these, the most common I have found are the following:

- **thorough analysis and understanding**
- **high-quality repetition**
- **super-slow practice**
- **"chunking" groups of notes into a single movement or concept**
- **small practice units**
- **expressive playing during all stages of practice**
- **using variety (loud, soft, fast, slow, etc.)**
- **visualization**

There are literally hundreds of books and papers on the "right" or "most effective" ways to practice, and each of them contains something I have left off this list. Even more importantly, none of the professional musicians I have known or researched have ever used every practice technique. Each finds the techniques that work best for her and uses them in contexts best suited to her use. In other words: personalized discipline. It is extremely important to recognize that we will do our children no favors by reading them a list of "best practice techniques" and criticizing them when they fail to use them effectively.

While researchers such as Ericsson, Dr. Robert A. Duke, Gary E. McPherson, and others have been studying the effects of deliberate practice on musicians, there have also been neurologists and psychologists such as Robert A. Bjork, George Bartzokis, and R. Douglas Fields studying what actually takes place physiologically inside the brain as we develop complex skills. Building new skills is, in essence, the act of building new and better neural pathways in our brains, creating new memories, and forming complex systems of mental representations that allow us to process patterns more quickly. Because this is a physiological process that involves the growth of millions of cells, we should expect it to take a long time. More importantly, we should understand that just like building muscle, building brainpower requires sustained effort and can be exhausting.

We can think of deliberate practice behaviors as the actions through which we are creating "talent." Most people think of the word *talent* as representing something with which we were born. Now, there is ample evidence to show that people who engage in deliberate practice techniques designed to improve performance can become vastly more adept in virtually any area of skill than people who showed "natural aptitude." As Ericsson puts it, "With deliberate practice, however, the goal is not just to reach your potential but to build it, to make things possible that were not possible before."

The problem with deliberate practice is that we are biologically engineered to hate it. It is a matter of survival that we conserve our energies for those activities most likely to ensure our survival. Or, put another way, our bodies cannot afford to waste energy developing complex neural pathways and building specific muscle groups unless there is an extremely powerful motivation to do so. When our body or brain is pushed to the outer limits of its abilities, it sends clear signals saying, "STOP! — This is too hard! You are using up valuable energy!" It sends us these signals in the form of resistance and exhaustion. When we are motivated enough to push through these signals, our bodies respond by redirecting energies to the affected areas to increase capacity for similar work in the future: bigger muscles, more lung capacity, more red blood cells, neural networks devoted to pattern detection — whatever is needed to accomplish the goal without running out of energy.

So, while learning new ideas or facts, exploring interesting topics, or engaging in activities within our comfort zone can be fun, real fundamental change is likely to require a level of effort that feels uncomfortable at best and is, most likely, occasionally frustrating and even repugnant. Of course, the *results* of all that struggle are what make it all worthwhile. When we develop physical, mental, and expressive abilities we never imagined possible and reflect on the path that led to that development, we can experience a level of satisfaction, joy, and even "fun" that was never possible for our old selves. The trick is to be able to remember that when we are in the midst of the struggle.

The goal of personalized discipline is to find out how to trigger intense engagement day after day for thousands of hours until we have not only transformed our bodies and minds, but also given ourselves the confidence that we can undertake future challenges using the same approach.

Transferring Music Lessons to Life Lessons

Most music teachers (including myself) are guilty of exaggerating the benefits of music to include everything that *might* be learned from musical experiences as though all of it will transfer automatically. We say, "Since musical rhythms are ratios, kids are learning ratios through playing music," or "Since learning music requires disciplined behavior, becoming a musician will inevitably make you a more disciplined person in all areas of your life." And while this might occasionally be the case, it is certainly not a given, as is obvious by the long list of excellent musicians with very little discipline in other areas of their lives.

Transfer of knowledge and skills from one context to another is difficult, and when it does occur, it doesn't always occur in a way that is helpful to the new situation. As Dr. Robert A. Duke puts it, "*Transfer is not reliably automatic....* In the abstract it may seem reasonable to expect that learners will effectively apply all of what we know and can do at every opportunity, [but] there is ample research ... that we often do not" (141).

We want our children not only to be able to transfer the musical skills they practice at home to band practice and the concert hall, but to be able to apply the lessons of personalized discipline, a learner's mindset, grit, and the highly effective learning techniques exemplified in deliberate practice more broadly to areas outside of their musical life. For example, I hope that my daughter might apply some of the practice techniques she learned on guitar, such as slow practice, to her tennis lessons, or apply the same discipline she brings to piano practice to her homework, or treat a bad grade on a test with the same learner's mindset and grit that she displayed after she failed to make the finals at the Guitar Foundation of America competition.

"Is it possible to teach in a way that increases the likelihood that students will use knowledge and skills beyond the context in which they were taught? ... The answer is a resounding yes," says Duke (154). There are several things we can do to facilitate transfer and make it more likely that our children will carry the lessons they have learned in music into the rest of their lives.

Transfer Works Best When Active and Conscious

Rather than simply expecting or hoping that our children will apply the lessons they have learned in music to other areas of their lives, we would do much better to talk about it explicitly as the primary goal of learning. "With prompting, transfer can improve quite dramatically," according to the National Research Council (66). Don't be afraid to say things like, "Making a schedule for practice really helped you get first chair on violin. I wonder if we could do the same for math?" or "We have so many fun games for mastering your guitar pieces, I wonder if we could do the same around reading?"

Transfer Works Best in a Variety of Contexts

If sight-reading is practiced at home in only one way, whether it is carefully clapping out the rhythms, writing in the fingering, or playing slowly enough so as to never make a mistake, then sight-reading will likely be extremely difficult in the context of band or any other ensemble where it is done differently. Mixing things up not only brings interest and variety to our practice, but also makes it more likely that we will be able to carry those skills into the rest of our lives. "When a subject is taught in multiple contexts, ... and includes examples that demonstrate wide application of what is being taught, people are more likely to abstract the relevant features of concepts and to develop a flexible representation of knowledge" (National Research Council 62).

Transfer Requires Deep Learning

An early study of students who learned the computer language LOGO showed no difference in problem-solving and logic abilities between students who had learned the computer language and those who had not. When the actual ability of the students was assessed, however, it was found that the former had not learned enough about the program to really know it in any depth. When students who had learned the program more thoroughly were tested, it was found that they were able to transfer the skills to new contexts.

> It is not merely the length of time or even the skill that is important; it is the depth of learning.

When it comes to music study, parents will often tell me that they want their child to experience the benefits to cognitive development, but there is no time to practice at home. My response is that merely signing up for music lessons is not like a magic fairy dust that will improve their focus, spatial reasoning, and discipline. It is only through the act of deep learning over many years that these concepts can be absorbed thoroughly enough to have an impact on other areas of life.

Furthermore, it is not merely the length of time spent studying or even the skill one can demonstrate that is important; it is the depth of learning. "Transfer is affected by the degree to which people learn with understanding rather than merely memorize sets of facts or follow a fixed set of procedures" (National Research Council 55).

Transfer Goes Both Ways

Our children bring a vast number of experiences and skills with them into their first lesson, though this is often overlooked. A wise teacher and parent will try to tap into these skills by learning a little about the child. Perhaps they play a sport and can understand how fluid motion helps make for unimpeded movement, or they are good at math and can understand rhythms more effectively as ratios, or they have shown discipline by adhering to a schedule of skating for one hour before school every day. Each of these things can be used to draw parallels between their music and their outside life. More importantly, as we saw above, using these skills in a variety of contexts makes it more likely they will apply them on their own in the future.

Considering How We Learn Aids Transfer

By critically examining their own unique learning processes, students are able to learn new concepts more independently and understand them more profoundly. In a musical context, this might mean making a plan to figure out which chords are already known from other songs, breaking the song into sections, practicing it slowly at first, or any number of other things. This process, called metacognition, has broad implications both for how we learn and how we transfer that learning. According to the National Research Council, "A metacognitive approach to teaching can increase transfer by helping students learn about themselves as learners in the context of acquiring content knowledge" (78).

A wonderfully fun way to get young children to think metacognitively is for the student to become the teacher. When they have to think about how to break down a concept so that someone else can understand it (perhaps a parent or sibling), then they end up thinking about how they themselves learned it.

4

THE THREE STAGES OF DEVELOPING DISCIPLINE

When my daughter was young and just beginning to study guitar, I was intent on helping her learn good practice habits, develop discipline, grit, and a learner's mindset. While my intentions were good, I very nearly killed her interest by pushing her too hard at too young an age. What I subsequently learned (hopefully in time to save her interest in music — she's still playing at age 13) was that interest needs to come first, followed by discipline, and only then can you pursue the intense practice that leads to exceptional skill. I wish I had had the opportunity to learn from some of the parents I have since interviewed for this book.

A Parent's Story

Jay had been an adult guitar student of mine for several years before he asked to sign up his daughter, Sarah, age seven, for lessons with my wife. Sarah would continue lessons for the next eight years, well into high school, reaching a solid intermediate level of play before deciding to stop lessons because school and marching band practice were taking up all her free time. Sarah's brother, Jake, also briefly took lessons, but decided not to continue, opting for trumpet once he reached middle school, and eventually going on to become a music major on that instrument. While neither Jake nor Sarah are currently playing professionally, both continue to play for fun, and, like their father, music is a big part of their adult lives. When I was looking for parents whose children have remained musical into adulthood to interview, Jay seemed an ideal candidate.

KS: *Why did you start your kids in music?*

Jay: I loved music, and I wanted my children to be able to share that love. Sarah took to it and loved to practice right away, but Jake wasn't interested at all in elementary school. For Sarah, learning to read music opened up a whole world of her mom's old piano books, and she would just take those and play through them for fun. When she got to middle school, she was able to get in the higher-level bands as a percussionist because of her reading and keyboard skills; then she made it into the top band in high school and even played in the marching band all the way through college as a math major.

KS: *How did you interact with them around practice at home?*

Jay: I mostly just set up the schedule and let them do it, but I could bring the hammer down if necessary. But most of the time they wanted to practice. You have to know your child, then help them to know themselves. With Sarah, sometimes that would mean encouraging her to put away the sight-reading and look at what Ms. Wendy had assigned, and other times, it meant suggesting she take a break if she was getting frustrated. I really enjoyed hearing the process and mostly preferred to let them make their own mistakes. I would compliment them on working through something, and sometimes they would just beam with pride. They always knew they could come to me for help, but usually I would deflect it back to the teacher. As they progressed in band, I became a "band parent," driving them around the state for competitions, going to concerts and games all the time, but it was fun for me.

KS: *What do you think made the biggest difference in their enjoying practice?*

Jay: I think that we stumbled into really good teachers for both instruments that made a good connection and built solid skills. They progressed faster than a lot of their peers, and they could see that and took pride in being first chair and things like that.

KS: *How much did they typically practice each week?*

Jay: At the start, it was just short practices each day, but as they reached middle school, it went up to 5–7 hours between the two instruments for Sarah and 10–15 hours a week in high school.

The Three Stages

While each family finds its unique relationship around music, Jay's experience of setting general boundaries but not interacting critically seems to be pretty common for those children who go on to enjoy making music as adults. This was also found to be the case in Benjamin Bloom's study of 24 professional pianists and was borne out in my interviews with professors of music at The University of Texas at Austin and adult amateurs active in community choirs and orchestras.

The Bloom study actually covered 120 "immensely talented individuals," including top pianists, sculptors, tennis players, swimmers, mathematicians, and neurologists, and included in-depth interviews with the parents as well as the "talented individuals." What emerges is a clear pattern of three phases of learning, which they group into "Early Years," "Middle Years," and "Later Years." My own experiences as a teacher and parent have mirrored that, but I have been referring to them as "Loving Practice," "Developing Discipline," and "Self-Motivation."

Three Stages of Developing Discipline

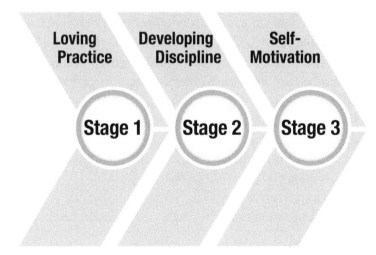

When I teach these stages in parent education classes, the first question I usually get is, "How long does each stage take?" The answer, of course, is that it varies. More importantly, it takes how long it takes, and we won't speed up the process by rushing. Developing love and interest can only be achieved if we are actually interested in what they enjoy before pressuring them to commit to a schedule of practice on their own. Developing discipline can only be achieved if we take the time to establish a steady routine without insisting on the most intense and rigorous practice techniques. If we restrict their time with friends and video games so that they can spend more time playing scales, studying music theory, and practicing slowly and carefully, odds are not in our favor that they will do so willingly.

Furthermore, once passion and discipline are well established, it doesn't mean they will remain solid. Motivating yourself isn't something you do once and are done. As one athlete commented, "It's like my mom said: You want to eat every day; you have to cook every day." Developing passion for an endeavor is a lifelong commitment to doing the things that keep you motivated. Developing discipline requires a lifelong commitment to learning what set of motivators, time-management tools, and accountability checks works for us at each age and stage of development (as well as which distractions we are willing to release).

The good news is that each stage is its own reward. If all your child does is develop a love of playing music and some solid good habits and then quits, *they still have a love of music that will allow them to return to it at any time!* If they love music and then develop a solid routine of practice but never advance to the use of the most rigorous training methods, *they still have learned how to be disciplined and value art in their lives!*

Most importantly, remember to enjoy the process. Our children want to play music that is beautiful and fun and delightful to all, especially their parents. If we take the time to appreciate that effort every day, we and our children will be the happier for it.

"How you climb a mountain is more important than reaching the top."
—**Yvon Chouinard**

5

STAGE ONE: LOVING PRACTICE AND ESTABLISHING HABITS

Research on peak performers in virtually all fields shows many of them share one thing in common: a positive early experience with their eventual field of expertise. If you think about it in the context of skill deriving from disciplined behavior rather than from talent, this makes perfect sense. The thousands of hours of painstaking, focused, and deliberate work required to reach the highest levels of skill in any field require an extremely high level of motivation. The same goes for adults who continue to play for fun and relaxation as amateur musicians. Most of them report loving music lessons as a child or growing up in a musical family.

So, whether we wish for our children to become concert pianists or simply to play for fun, the evidence would seem to indicate that the best start is a happy one. In time, it will be up to them to decide whether or not to practice music with the intensity required to achieve greatness, but if we give them a joyful start, they will have the fuel they need either to ignite that greatness or simply enjoy a relaxing hobby. Yes, it is also important for students to develop a solid foundation of technical and musical skills so that they may easily progress to music with which they can express themselves as they grow, but the primary focus should be on developing a deep love of music and enjoying playing. I always tell parents that I can fix the technique of a child who is motivated, but motivating a discouraged child with flawless technique is much harder (though not impossible).

Our goal for the first few years of music lessons should be simply to make playing great music a regular and joyful part of our child's life. If we can achieve that (and that is no small feat), and our child's teacher has given him pieces through which he has developed a solid foundation and strong attachment to learning music, we will be in the best possible position to begin the transition toward disciplined, focused learning.

The best advice I can give parents and teachers is this: *As much as possible, make these early years a series of meaningful goals resulting in delightful musical experiences.* If the child has a personal connection to what he is attempting to accomplish, adequate guidance from a teacher, and a supportive structure at home, there is a high likelihood that he will experience a profoundly satisfying musical moment upon achieving his goal. Repeat this process a number of times, and there is a good chance that he will develop a deep love of music. It is this love that will provide the energy necessary to engage in the challenging process of becoming a disciplined human being, capable of choosing the thorny path of self-improvement over the easy path of pleasure-seeking.

Audrey's Story

The first thing you notice about Audrey is a kind of guileless enthusiasm and inexhaustible attention to whatever activity is going on. Beginning lessons at age six, she impressed me with how long she could stay focused on any task I gave her. Whether we were playing "Ring around the Rosie" or technical exercises on the fingerboard, she was willing and eager.

Since both her parents worked full-time, Audrey was brought to the lesson by her nanny, Ms. Sandy, who recorded every lesson to play for her dad at home. Initially, we learned every pitch and rhythm concept through songs and games that we played in the lesson and then were repeated at home. Though Audrey learned quickly, I noticed she didn't always remember the songs or concepts the next week. A parent-teacher conference revealed that, despite loving the guitar and being eager to play it more often, some weeks she wasn't able to practice more than once or twice, due to a variety of things, including after-school activities and work schedules. Adjustments were made, including a practice schedule, and the speed of learning skyrocketed.

Over the summer, Audrey performed in her first recital, and I was surprised to see how nervous she was. She wouldn't smile or look at anyone, and it seemed she could hardly breathe. "Audrey," I said, "you know this piece, and you are going to be just fine." On stage, she looked like a statue, but she played like an angel. Afterward, the smiles returned, and she was her usual happy self.

At the end of the first year, Audrey passed her Level 1 Musical Journey* exam, which tested her ear-training, sight-reading, technique, and pieces. Soon after that, she performed her first "Home Concert," including a lovely composition of her own, "Bluebird in the Sky." As we were warming, up I could see she was having trouble breathing again, but I assured her she would be fine. We had been through this program a dozen times, and she knew it backward and forward. Despite a little tightness, she did fine, and then she had a blast playing with her friends all over the house.

Not long ago, Audrey performed "Moon River" at her parent's 10th anniversary party. It was the song they had danced to at their wedding, and it was her namesake, Audrey Hepburn, who had made it famous in *Breakfast at Tiffany's*. What I noticed this time, though, was laughter and smiles leading up to her performance. Maybe it was just that the focus was on her parents, or maybe she is getting used to the stage; we won't know until her next performance, but progress is progress. Of course, the performance was a huge success, and Audrey got to be an important part of a beautiful moment with her family.

Because Audrey has had so many positive and powerful experiences with the guitar, her commitment to the instrument has only grown. Now her willingness to work even harder than before to understand challenging musical concepts, to read music, to work on the difficult task of playing fluid lines on the guitar is so high that her potential is whatever she wants it to be.

> For children to develop discipline, we need to start with developing love for music.

Love – Habit – Discipline

We want our children to develop discipline, but we need to start with developing love. Once there is a high level of enjoyment and the child

---

*"Musical Journey" is a creative achievement system we invented at our music school, which tests all-around music skills while helping kids set ambitious but attainable creative and performance goals.

expresses a desire to play harder music, we can gradually begin teaching them the skills of personalized discipline.

Using these skills, they will realize their potential is unlimited because they can confidently encounter challenges, systematically break them down, and develop the skills needed to overcome them. Their lives will therefore be balanced, happy, and filled with success. — *If only it were that easy!*

Parenting is a difficult and confusing job. There is a seemingly endless supply of advice on what to do and how to do it with the implication that if we do it wrong, we will scar our children forever. Rest assured that I have no intention of adding to that interminable list. There will not be a flashing red light that tells you when your child is ready to take on more responsibility or when they are bored with the easy, fun pieces that delighted them earlier. We simply need to commit to trying new things, noticing when it helps and when it makes things worse, making corrections, and moving on. Sometimes it will be messy and frustrating, and other times it will be divine and satisfying beyond any possible expression.

While we all share common needs, the essence of personalized discipline is discovering and utilizing that which works to motivate us, which is as unique as each of us is. The same is true for loving practice: All children should start with a positive experience of music at home, in lessons, and in practice, but what this will look like for each individual child may differ dramatically. That is why it is helpful to have a list of "practice tips" handy. We can relax knowing that if the approach we are currently using doesn't work, there are a dozen other approaches we can try. As you read through this section, there may be things that could work well for your family, and there will certainly be many things that won't. The goal is to find what works for your child and help her to notice how she can acquire the ability to motivate herself to build exceptional skill and overcome difficult challenges by tapping into her own unique motivational system.

Before we delve further into how to develop a loving relationship with music, I want to present one simple formula to any parent struggling with creating an effective practice environment at home. I know I have said that each person must find his own personalized set of motivators, but the following three steps will solve 90 percent of all practice struggles at home:

1. Set a clear practice schedule that you can stick to 75 to 80 percent of the time.
2. Remove roadblocks (distractions such as screens, power struggles, an overwhelming schedule, hunger, or fatigue).
3. Find a special personal connection (culturally significant music, friends with whom to play music, a particular style of music).

Growing into a disciplined and expressive musician will take more than using the three points above, but, in my experience, they can provide the fastest solution to conflict surrounding practice.

The Three Pillars in Stage One

Learner's Mindset

I can remember the first time I drew my fingers lightly across the strings of my father's 12-string guitar in an old storage barn. The sound seemed to float through the air and hang there along with the dust dancing in the sunlight flowing through the broken slats in the ceiling. For me, it was pure magic, and I knew that this was something I wanted to do.

If we are lucky, children come to the learning process excited by the prospect of making music on this mysterious and magical thing we call a piano, or guitar, or voice, or whatever they have been drawn to. This excitement can translate into the curiosity, problem-solving, and patience required to learn if only we (or the world) don't get in the way. Unfortunately, there are more ways to quash a child's interest than I can count — from pushing him to learn too fast to moving so slowly and pedantically that he becomes bored, from thrusting him in front of an audience before he's ready to over-protecting him from taking risks. But of all the dangers teachers and parents can pose to a child's learner's mindset, none is so great (nor so common) at this stage as telling him that he is "talented."

When little Mikka comes homes after her first lesson and proudly plays "Hot Cross Buns" on the black keys of the piano, it is nearly impossible for most parents (including myself) not to comment on her amazing abilities in such a short amount of time. But, as was noted earlier, this sets up at least two important and powerful expectations in the mind of the child:

1. Learning new pieces will be easy.
2. I'm smart and talented because I can learn fast.

Now, when she goes to learn the next piece and there is some difficulty, she is likely to wonder, "Maybe I'm not so talented after all. Maybe this isn't for me." More importantly, she is giving only half her attention to the process of learning and playing. The other half is devoted to looking for praise or other feedback because that is how she will know if she is "talented" or not, and we have signaled that being talented is the highest status we can give to a musician.

The mother of one student I had many years ago would sit in the lesson and croon over his every note, "Oh Benjamin, that was SO beautiful!" He would beam and look happy, but what I began to notice was that he was always looking toward his mother after every note to receive the praise. As he grew older, I asked his mom to let us work alone for part of the lesson, and I noticed him scrutinizing my face for signs of approval. Unfortunately, it is extremely difficult to both play the guitar and read your teacher's facial expressions! I often jokingly tell my students, "The music is not written on my forehead!" It is virtually impossible for most people to give up a natural and largely unconscious behavior such as praising the talent of a child who has just played something beautifully. But if we make a plan ahead of time, it may be possible to replace that reaction with another one. My suggestion is to learn to ask questions rather than hand out praise. This draws the child's focus toward the music and the process of learning and away from our judgment of him. "How did you learn that?" we can ask, or, "Do you like this piece? Why?" or, "Ooh, I like that! Can you teach it to me?"

I read Dr. Dweck's work a few years prior to the birth of my daughter, Mei Yin, and my wife and I vowed to scrupulously avoid using talent-based praise. Her entire childhood, we were quick to recognize effort and even privately scolded grandparents not to praise her intelligence. Nevertheless, she has shown some signs of being prone to fixed-mindset thinking, such as wanting to learn pieces quickly without exploring solutions to challenges. Of course, this is completely normal, and it hasn't stopped her from becoming a fine musician. Nevertheless, as I have reflected upon the times she has had an extreme resistance to slowing down, getting curious, and solving problems, I have wondered if perhaps I have been projecting an unconscious desire for her to display exceptional talent, even though I wasn't expressing it overtly. She would overhear me say that another student had sung beautifully in tune on the very first lesson and later would ask me if *her* singing was in tune. I have noticed that since I have let go of my desire for my students (including my daughter) to show exceptional talent, they, in turn, have shown greater curiosity and willingness to work toward a meaningful goal. In essence, by releasing my interest in "talent," I have helped my students become more talented.

What of the child who does not bring eagerness and curiosity to the first lesson, but instead starts music with resistance, fear, or even a refusal to learn? There are some teachers who will accept only students who have chosen that particular instrument themselves for the very reason that a learner's mindset is so critical to success. Better to go learn something that interests you than to waste your time and mine with something you hate, they say. I understand this point of view, but I have seen so many children turn their attitude around with the right teacher, the right music, and the right practice environment at home that I am loath to give up on these kids out of hand. There may be many good reasons for their feelings of resistance, and it is our job to listen, make adjustments, set boundaries, and see if there is a path forward.

For some children, the fear of judgment is so intense that even making the slightest effort toward learning is unbearable. This is often expressed through violent exclamations of "I hate playing piano!" or "This is STUPID!" While it is possible that the child's environment has led to this extreme fixed mindset (the belief that our self-worth is based on our fixed abilities rather than an attitude of learning and growing), I believe some kids are simply born with a greater sensitivity to the judgment of others, making it exceptionally difficult for them to concentrate on learning for fear they will be judged as incompetent.

I feel a particular kinship with these children as I write this book. Being an avid reader all my life, but never a writer, I have many times been filled with self-judgment about the quality of my writing.

I re-read passages and find them to be stale, pedantic, and clumsy. Sometimes this feeling is so intense that I have a visceral reaction to sitting down at the computer to write. My chest would tighten up, and I felt I would rather be anywhere else in the world at that moment (I returned emails, got a *lot* of house cleaning done, and put together several pieces of IKEA™ furniture in this process). Fortunately, on the good days I was able to apply the lessons I had learned from practice. I made it fun (put on my favorite music, made a latte, set a cookie in the other room for when I was done). I followed a schedule. I set up accountability. Most of all, I reminded myself that this is a learning process and, if I wanted to, I could always write a second edition once I got parent feedback.

Most children, when placed in an environment of creative commitment, one that says, "We're sticking with this, and together we'll find a creative way to make it fun," begin to fall in love with music over a period of time. When we work together to find the right combination of music they love, a learning style that works for them, and a practice strategy they can stick to, I feel that something truly meaningful and powerful has transpired. That is the ultimate reward of teaching.

Developing Grit

Remember Duckworth's admonition: *"Before hard work comes play."* This is the period of ignition, of falling in love and of experiencing enough early success that there is a hope of future successes. The transition to the "desirable difficulty" upon which children can "cut their teeth," as they say in the music business, should come only after motivation and strong habits are securely in place.

A major aspect of grit is self-control or willpower. Much research has been done on our ability to exercise self-control in different situations. You may have heard of the now-famous experiment where children were told if they could sit at a table in front of a marshmallow for ten minutes without eating it, they could have two marshmallows. The videos of these children struggling to control themselves through distraction or hiding the marshmallow are priceless. Through studies like these, as well as what we now know about brain development (not to mention the common sense of parents everywhere), we know that self-control is slow to develop. It is hardly present in toddlers, and the part of the brain associated with self-control (the prefrontal cortex) does not completely finish developing until our mid-twenties.

This is why it is more effective to focus our attention at this stage on developing healthy habits than withstanding difficult challenges. Because habits automate our behavior, they do not draw upon limited resources of willpower and self-control. Furthermore, establishing good habits early on gives our children a powerful tool for self-improvement for the rest of their lives. The habit of daily practice, like the habit of reading books, is akin to starting a savings account with compounding interest. Every day their skills grow stronger, and these skills, in turn, become a powerful reward that reinforces the habit of practice.

Habits can be reliably established through a trigger, a consistent behavior, and a reward.

Habit Formation: Trigger, Action, Reward

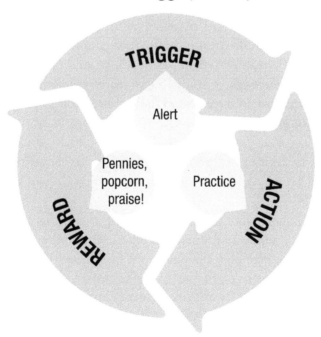

There is some research that indicates that a habit typically takes 21 days of consistent repetition to establish. It is not surprising then, that in my surveys of parents, a schedule and a practice chart to earn rewards are the number-one tools used for early success.

Unfortunately, it only takes three to four days of breaking a routine to disrupt a habit. Travel, illness, soccer games, guests — the list of possible disruptions is endless. This is life, and it is completely normal. The important thing to remember is to expect some additional resistance to practice after a disruption in the routine and to have to meet it with additional motivation (more on this later).

Deliberate Practice

As we have established, significant, qualitative change requires a level of effort to build neural pathways, muscles, and habits that few are willing to expend. It might seem, then, that there is little chance that a young child with a short attention span, weak fingers, and a strong desire for immediate gratification would be capable of this level of intense work. However, there is a special opportunity for young beginners with parents and teachers who are willing to put in the work to make the challenges of deliberate practice into games. With the assistance of a trained teacher and a dedicated parent, some of the most powerful practice techniques can be done with small children as young as three or four years old. All it takes is a clear goal and the willingness to "gamify" the activity.

> Young children are often more willing to do repetitive tasks than older children — but only if we make it into a game.

Kids (especially young kids) are willing to do the most intensely focused activity when it is turned into a game. Remember the boy mentioned in the first chapter who didn't like repetitions? His father shared with me the rules of the game he created for this child: The son needed to score 100 points on a particular phrase before he could move on, *but* each try was worth 1–10 points, depending on how well he played — *and* he could double his points if he did it with his eyes closed. The father reported that his son rarely had to play a passage more than five or six times and actually enjoyed the challenge of playing super slowly with his eyes closed. This boy also went on to take second prize in a national competition at age 11.

Perhaps it has happened with some child somewhere, but I personally have never witnessed a young child engaging in deliberate practice in the absence of positive support from a teacher and parent. I have witnessed (and even been guilty of) parents getting angry at their children for not doing good practice on their own. "If you're not fixing your mistakes, you are just wasting your time!" I am ashamed to say that I have said these very words and heard of many parents saying something similar to their young children. The problem is that we just don't realize how intense our resistance to real change is. I sometimes wish I could challenge every parent to work on carefully improving some detailed aspect of their lives before accusing their child of being lazy.

The number-one advantage of an early start is that young children are often willing to do the repetitive tasks required for improvement that older children find boring, *but only if we make it into a game*. With that in mind, here are ...

10 Games You Can Play with Your Child

1. FUN COUNTERS
Place three to ten fun things he can earn (pennies, pieces of popcorn, pencil holders — anything small he loves) on one side and move one over for every successful attempt. As he gets better, you can challenge him by taking a counter back for every mistake or even adding a tougher rule, such as having to make three to five successful attempts in a row. But remember, the point is to have fun, so shoot for the sweet spot of 50 to 80 percent success. Above 80 percent success becomes boring. Below 50 percent success becomes frustrating.

2. DICE FOR REPETITION
When I tell my students they need to repeat a phrase three times, they groan. If I offer to let them roll a die to determine the number of repetitions, with the choice of a 6-, 10-, or 20-sided die, I don't know why, but they usually pick the 20 and hope for a high number. Even

the ones who pick the 6-sided die, hoping to roll a one, are still more willing to repeat the phrase when they roll a six — because it's a game.

3. WHO CAN PLAY THE SLOWEST?

This works only if the parent can learn to play the instrument a little, too (which isn't that hard at the beginning). Playing super slowly is one of the most effective learning strategies in any discipline. If you say, "Slow down! You're practicing your mistakes" (as I have), your child will likely play angrily. But if she plays this game, then when you play slowly, on her turn she will play *super* slowly to beat you.

4. WEIRDO PRACTICE

How many different ways can you play this phrase? Loudly, softly, quickly, slowly, smoothly, choppily, angrily, sadly … upside down? Another advanced practice technique is to mix it up. Breakthroughs, memorization, and physical control all come from looking at things from different angles.

5. TIMERS AND STOPWATCHES

Literally everything is more fun when you are trying to beat your old time: reading notes, technique exercises, how many mistakes you can fix in under a minute. Of course, we don't want to reward sloppy practice, so it counts only if it is good, but kids get that. If you are timing how many shots you can make in basketball in five minutes, they wouldn't want you to count misses.

6. YOU TEACH ME

Articulating the exact actions needed for success is one of the behaviors in which great practicers of any skill succeed. It helps them to visualize exactly the sequence of actions they need to take to be successful. Many parents find asking — or even paying — their child to teach them helps him to be more willing to practice and more effective in his practice.

7. DRAW FROM A HAT

As a memory test, we can put the titles of pieces or phrases of an individual piece into a hat and let the child draw them out to decide what to perform. Some teachers even get so creative as to write the titles on magnets and then allow the child to fish them out of a "pond." Whatever the procedure, we know that testing our memory is the fastest way to improve it. One study showed that reviewing test materials once, and then testing a child's memory of the material three times was 50 percent more effective than studying the material ten times.

8. FREEZE AND THINK
On a cue or the word "Freeze!" the child must stop and say what is coming next in the music. This is particularly helpful when trying to break a bad habit such as a wrong note, wrong fingering, or difficult shift. Dr. Duke and his colleagues observed in multiple studies that expert practicers are much more likely to pause and think prior to a difficult section (317).

9. TELL A STORY OR DRAW A PICTURE
Expert practicers are more likely to visualize their music in creative, nonlinear ways. Fortunately, young children are frequently better at creative imagery than adults, so all it takes is a little nudge. To ensure that the representation helps them truly represent their piece of music, it can be helpful to ask them to describe each of the sections of the piece prior to starting to make a story about it: "At the beginning, the notes are going up in fast little patterns. In the middle, we have all of these long, low, smooth notes, and then the beginning part comes back again at the end. If this were a story about our dog, what do you think would be happening?"

10. SING THE NOTES WHILE MOVING TO THE MELODY
Feeling the arc of the music within your own body can help you to play more expressively. Dancing can help you identify where the strong and weak beats lie.

The Importance of Skill Development in the Early Years

While the first few years of study should be all about "having fun" and falling in love with music, it is also important that the child develop some solid musical skills at the same time. Never at the *expense* of enjoying music, but *while* enjoying music. Most of the adult musicians, both amateur and professional whom I interviewed, stated that being able to read music, learn pieces without too much physical difficulty, and understand how music works made learning music easier in middle school when they started to get busy. For my own daughter, having played in ensembles, accompanied singers, sung in choir, improvised, composed, and performed in many

Photo courtesy of Luis Diaz

contexts before she was ten years old has made it easy for her to join in any new musical opportunity that comes along. If a tune pops into her head, she just goes to the piano and plays it (lately whenever she walks by the piano she plucks out the melody that played whenever someone died in the movie *The Hunger Games* — I'm not really sure what that's about).

Now imagine a child who has played guitar for four years but can muster only two or three chords, can't read music, and can play only the melody to "Ode to Joy." When this child reaches middle school, how is she going to use these skills to interact with her peers, build self-esteem, or express herself? With the increased demands upon her time for homework and other extracurriculars, she is almost certain to drop guitar in favor of something that provides more personal satisfaction.

Don't get me wrong: If I had to choose between a student who has terrible technique, can't read, or play by ear, but still loves music, and a skillful student who hates music because it has been beaten into him,

I would prefer the former. It is easier to rebuild skills in someone with enthusiasm than it is to build enthusiasm in someone who is highly skilled. But we shouldn't have to choose! As Dr. Timothy Woolsey puts it, "When a student starts to see progress, that in itself is a great motivation. Effective practice leads to progress. Progress leads to a greater desire to practice well."

In my experience, progress by itself is only part of the equation to creating a positive cycle of practice, but it is an important part. As we have seen, true progress is extremely challenging and requires the whole host of unique motivators that make up each child's portfolio of personalized discipline techniques.

Motivation *vs.* Resistance: A Model for Developing Interest and Overcoming Obstacles

In developing a love of music, it can be helpful to think about our ability to engage joyfully in terms of two countervailing forces: *motivation* and *resistance*.

Resistance is simply a list of things that get in the way of engaging in a desired activity with love and enthusiasm. Distractions, not enough time, or a broken instrument are examples of external forces that might get in the way of practice. Lack of interest, lack of sleep, boredom, feeling insecure, or a lack of finger strength might be examples of internal challenges. A very useful and eye-opening exercise is to make a list (with your child's input) of her external and internal causes of resistance to practicing. Try not to judge yourself when making the list, but rather strive to make an objective inventory of what is getting in the way. Until any of us have a clear picture of what is really true for us, we have no way of creating the life we desire. Making a list is simply a tool to help us think creatively about how we can find time and energy to do what we want.

> "Taking stock of our motivations can help us increase our awareness of them and improve their effectiveness."

Similarly, motivation is simply a list of all the things that help us engage in joyful, effective music-making. For example, we might list a desire to do well on an upcoming concert, loving the sound of the instrument, wanting to get better, or wanting to learn a favorite song. Taking stock of our motivations can help us increase our awareness of them and improve their effectiveness.

The motivation/resistance paradigm is just one way of looking at why we engage (or fail to engage) in disciplined behavior. Of course, practicing effectively, with focus and the desire to improve, is another thing altogether, and I will cover this in the coming chapters. Initially, however, simply getting our kids to engage with the instrument willingly will allow them to build their confidence and love of music so they can later learn the skills of deep practice.

Successfully managing our motivation and resistance isn't a matter of having more things on the motivation side than the resistance side. One might have a hundred little reasons to play guitar, but if you don't actually have a functioning guitar, that one block will likely prevent you from learning. Conversely, the great Django Reinhardt had every reason to quit once his hand had been so badly burned that he was left with only one fully working finger and another stub. Nevertheless, his love of jazz, need to support his family, and many other things led him to persevere with such intensity that he changed the landscape of jazz guitar forever and produced his greatest recordings after the accident.

Writing out a Motivation and Resistance Chart should help us

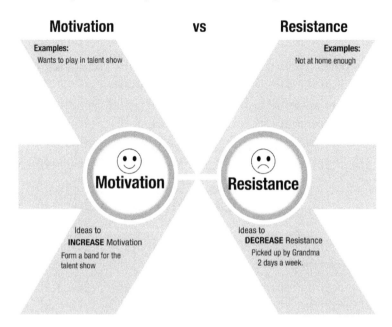

to strengthen and increase our child's motivations and discover and resolve his sources of resistance. If we find that his *only* motivation is not to get in trouble and his resistance is a long list of challenges — from a poor instrument, to not liking his teacher, to endless boring exercises, and too much homework — then we know we have some serious problem-solving to do.

My own Motivation and Resistance Chart on practicing guitar looks like this at this time:

MOTIVATION

- Love for my music
- Desire to play well in my lesson
- Belief that I can create a unique concert experience for audience
- Terrific feeling after a good practice
- Love of sitting down with a cup of coffee in a quiet room with my guitar

RESISTANCE

- Physical pain from spine injury
- Insufficient mental energy after work, writing book, parenting, etc.
- Distractions: news, sports, and social media
- No accountability

Possible Ways to Increase Motivation	*Possible Ways to Decrease Resistance*
• Ensure similar music is playing at home and in the car. • Schedule more frequent lessons. • Schedule more concerts. • Schedule more quiet time.	• Find a new chiropractor / physical therapist. • Practice in the morning, while fresh. • Unplug the modem. • Schedule more lessons and concerts.

The Six C's of Motivation

In my Loving Practice, Developing Discipline workshops, I share what I call "The Six C's of Motivation":

Six C's of Motivation

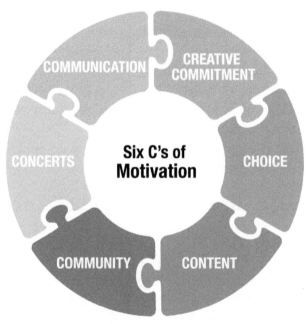

Creative Commitment

If discipline is the process of learning how to motivate ourselves, how can we better engage our children in this process day after day so that they grow their self-awareness and eventually carry that

68

discipline into adulthood? For myself, my daughter, and the parents of my students, the best answer has been what I call "creative commitment," which is embodied by the motto, "We're sticking with this, and together we will find a creative way to make it fun."

We want to communicate to our children that if there is a problem, we will work with them to find a creative solution. Practicing is hard. Everyone who is any good at music has wanted to give up from time to time. Communicating clear expectations of commitment is essential not only to success in music, but to building the type of character that is successful in life. At the same time, we are not saying we will force the child to endure an experience they hate. What we are saying is this: "You have chosen to do something challenging and worthwhile. What can we do to make it more enjoyable and successful?" When your child knows that you will support her to make things better and you will not give up on creating a positive learning environment no matter how challenging, she will be much more likely to engage with you in finding ways to be successful. This process of seeking ways to make challenging tasks enjoyable is the process of learning to be disciplined.

That is the creative part of the process, but why is commitment such an important element in success? Why can't we simply make the learning process so much fun that they will never want to quit? It isn't merely that anything worthwhile will be so challenging that we eventually encounter frustration (though that is part of it), it is also that the attitude of commitment affects our thinking and motivation from the very beginning and all the way through.

I have personally seen this in hundreds of students. Those whose parents begin with an attitude of "trying it out" to see if their child has an interest show little or no willingness to try different ways of finding motivation. Families who begin with the attitude "Music is just something we do because it is a joyful and important part of life" are willing to experiment with many approaches to practice until they find something that works for them. Of course, the development of musical skill is only one of the benefits of this outcome.

Everyone knows that it requires effort and commitment over a long period of time to achieve meaningful results. What is less well known is that *an unwavering commitment to a decision or course of action can actually increase our happiness and satisfaction with that decision.* When people reserve the right to change their mind, they have a tendency to notice all the flaws in their current situation. Conversely, when we are stuck with our lot, as Gilbert and Ebert point out, "People have a special talent for restructuring their views of outcomes so that those outcomes are experienced more positively" (503).

What this means for music study is that parents who tell their child that if he is unhappy in the lesson, he can always switch to a different teacher, different instrument, or quit altogether are making it vastly more likely that their child actually *will* be unhappy. In one study of photography, student researchers asked students to choose between two of their photographic prints to take home. Half the participants were told they could change their mind later about which one they chose (the "changeable" group), while the other half were told that their decision was final ("unchangeable"). In a subsequent evaluation, the "changeable" group appreciated the photograph they had originally chosen less than they did initially, while the unchangeable group saw significant increase in how they rated their photograph. Interestingly, when later asked, the majority of participants in the "unchangeable" group said that they would have preferred to be offered the choice to change. What this suggests is that most of us do a rather poor job of predicting how we will feel about an experience in the future. We mistakenly believe that keeping our options open will lead to greater happiness, while the opposite is often the case.

It isn't that the ability to change our minds is always a bad thing. Particularly in circumstances where we do not have enough information and the consequences of a poor decision could be catastrophic, it is certainly in our best interest to reserve the right to change our decision once we have the information we need. Consider any house-flipping show on HGTV™ where they decide to purchase a fixer-upper sight-unseen that looks great on paper, only to find out that it needs $20,000 in foundation repairs and a brand-new plumbing system, causing them to actually lose money on the resale after the renovation. With music lessons, however, where trust, engagement, and the belief in the possibility of success are crucial to making progress, it is important, once we *have* gathered the necessary information, to commit ourselves fully to the process of learning.

For this reason, I recommend that parents tell their kids, "We're sticking with this, and together we will find a creative way to make it fun." This signals to the child that he should settle in and become an active part of creating a positive outcome, but that he is not condemned to a lifetime of boredom and drudgery. Furthermore, commitment to learning music does not mean commitment to a particular instrument or teacher whose approach isn't working for your child or your family. I always tell every family I work with, "I want you to love music, and if that means finding another teacher, another instrument, or another school because I haven't found the right way to help you, then you absolutely should do that."

Choice

Fostering commitment is not the same as barring all choices. Perhaps the strongest desire of all is the desire to be free to make our own decisions about what we do and how we do it. Of course, running out into a busy street is not something we are prepared to let our children choose, but it is helpful to understand that resistance to our plans for their success is reasonable and normal.

> When children get to choose how they are musical, they become more excited about music.

Ideally, practicing music becomes practicing to be a happy, successful human being, and this means practicing making good choices in our lives. In the following paragraphs, I outline several ways in which children can engage in appropriate choices at every level of their musical development, from which instrument they play to when, what, and how much they practice.

When people feel they have agency in their own lives, they are much more likely to be interested in what they are doing. When our children get to choose how they are musical, their minds become more excited about the music, and therefore they learn more joyfully and more effectively. Our job is to help them make healthy choices by the way we present the options. If we ask, "Would you like to join the family for a bowl of ice cream, or would you rather practice piano?"

we can be sure of one particular outcome. But if instead we offer the choice, "Do you want to practice before or after your bath tonight?" we are likely to get quite a different response.

CHOOSING THE RIGHT INSTRUMENT

As the director of a music school, I am frequently asked, "On which instrument would it be best for my child to start?" Early on in my teaching career, I would always answer, "Whichever one they choose. All instruments provide a wonderful vehicle for developing a full musical understanding, and all instruments require dedication, hard work, and passion. Therefore, you want your child to start out as motivated as possible."

Over time, however, I have tempered this response to take into account the whole family and the physical limitations of the child. Some instruments (most of the wind family, for example) cannot physically be played by children under the age of nine. Other instruments (most strings) require very complex physical coordination at the early stages,

which can only be mastered with intense and direct assistance from a parent. Unless you are willing to put in the time and energy to guide your child on how to hold the violin, grasp the bow, place the fingers, etc., you might want to wait until your child is at least eight or nine to start violin.

Of course, a great teacher will guide the parent on how to best help their child practice. On the other hand, a teacher who does not sequence the challenges of learning any instrument will make even the "easiest" instrument a chore.

Not all instruments work for all families. Perhaps you don't have the room in your house or car for a harp. Perhaps you have grandparents in

Photo courtesy of Romy Hoover

the house who don't like loud drumming. On the other hand, perhaps you already have a piano in the house and can't afford to go out and buy another instrument at this time. As in all choices, we want to offer options that are likely to be successful, provide clear feedback upon the limits of what we can do, and then, when they have made the decision, provide the support they need to be successful.

CHOOSING WHEN TO PRACTICE

The choice of when to practice is one of the most important steps in creating a regular habit of playing music. If you have to "find time" or "remember" to practice each day, odds are good that you won't. On the other hand, many children resent being told unexpectedly, "Time to practice! Put away your toys and get out your violin."

I am not naive enough to suggest that just because you made an agreement during the lesson that Johnny would practice after dinner each night, that this will magically make practice easy and fun. If Johnny got to help decide between several options (all of which worked for the whole family), however, it will reduce one element of the power struggle that I have seen all too often.

Additionally, establishing a healthy routine allows us to harness the natural ability of the brain to prepare to learn effectively. Remember, it takes 21 days to establish a habit and only three to four days to break one. Understanding this can help take some of the stress out of the first 21 days after a break when you are aware that there is going to be resistance to sitting down to concentrate. Stay the course and be confident in the knowledge that once the routine is reestablished, you are much more likely to experience willing and even joyful engagement. When there is resistance, the fact that the child chose the time can be very helpful, for example, "I know practicing is challenging, but you chose 7:30 as your practice time, and in our family, we honor our commitments. I am, however, happy to help you make the practice more fun. What can I do to help?"

CHOOSING WHAT TO PRACTICE

Generally, the teacher will have provided most of the practice material, but this doesn't mean there is no room for choice! The child can certainly choose the order of activities in her practice, and with many teachers, their students can choose whether to spend some time improvising, creating variations, practicing half their pieces one day and the other half the next. More importantly, a good teacher will have several pieces that are all the same level and will ask the child to make choices about which pieces she would like to learn. Among the explanations I hear from parents who have switched their children to my academy, not getting to pick their pieces is one of the top reasons why their children were unhappy with their previous teacher.

CHOOSING HOW LONG TO PRACTICE

It is important that children practice enough to be able to see their own progress from week to week. Otherwise, they (as well as their parents) will start to doubt whether it is worth practicing at all. Just like all the other decisions we are helping our children make, this one should be based on a reasonable understanding of what they themselves would like to achieve. In her early years of study, I would ask my daughter, "How many times do you think you need to practice each piece per day in order for it to get better?" She always answered with a number that was much too high, and we had to discuss how she might lose interest and start to make mistakes after ten times. Other students might say, "One" or even "Zero!" but they almost always end up deciding that anything less than three times per day will not be enough.

The important step here, though, is helping them to decide. The fact that they have agency in the decision process not only helps them participate willingly in their instrument practice, but also helps them practice decision making. How many times do you need to do anything well before you can reasonably expect to do it well consistently?

TOO MUCH CHOICE

"Choice is essential to autonomy, which is absolutely fundamental to well-being. Healthy people want and need to direct their own lives. On the other hand, the fact that some choice is good doesn't necessarily mean that more choice is better.... There is a cost to having an overload of choice" (Schwartz 3).

As parents we have all experienced how easily our children can become overwhelmed by 32 ice cream flavors or the toy aisle in

Target™ when they have to choose just one. Similarly, teachers can make the mistake of playing a dozen pieces for the child to choose from, and parents can ask the child to pick whether she wants to play for grandma, record for Facebook, play her favorite song, or work on the newest piece. In my experience, my daughter worked best with deciding between two acceptable choices rather than a hundred.

> *MUSIC LESSON TO LIFE LESSON*
> Including children in the decision-making process teaches them how to think critically about what is best for them so that they can make good choices independently down the line.

Content

When we first opened our music school, I thought the primary motivator for my employees would be salary. It took many failures to come to understand that while people need to make enough to feel valued, their primary source of motivation comes from feeling that the content of their work is worthwhile. It was then that I stopped looking for teachers with impressive performing resumes and began looking for teachers who were excited by making a difference in the lives of their students.

The same is true for children. They will work tirelessly on something they view as having value in their lives, but resist or even rebel against activities that have no meaning for them, no matter how we attempt to manipulate them through punishment or reward. This is why it is so important to pick the right music for each student, or at least, give him a powerful reason to focus on what he is learning. If a student loves his music and especially if he can see how his music helps him relate to his world, he will not only have a great reason to practice, he will do so with the kind of interest and excitement that leads to genuine improvement.

Many teachers either utilize a relatively short list of pieces for every student or stick to a method book for all their teaching. Most Suzuki teachers, for example, will stick to the pieces in the Suzuki method (though many good ones have "expansion pieces" for older students or what they call "pre-Twinkle" pieces for younger children not ready to begin Book One). Having a short list of teaching pieces allows the teacher to effectively prepare the student for nearly every technical and musical challenge the pieces may present, and this is a HUGE advantage. As someone who has suffered long-term physical damage as the result of poor technical training, I can completely understand the desire to have an approach to teaching that is reliable, well thought out, and well prepared each step of the way.

> One of the best motivators for any work is feeling that the *content* of that work is worthwhile.

From my point of view, limiting a child's repertoire to merely the music the teacher is prepared to teach exacts far too great a cost in motivation and self-discovery. We would never consider teaching young children to read using Chaucer or giving older remedial readers the old "Dick and Jane" books (at least I hope we wouldn't). I believe an expert teacher can achieve balance here: having several, if not dozens of, exciting pieces ready for each age and skill level to choose from, all of which effectively teach the skills the student is ready to learn, while also being open to including music meaningful to the child or relevant to the child's culture and/or family. This does not mean that the parent and child should dictate what is taught in the lesson, but a good teacher will seek out what interests the child and find ways to incorporate that music or style into the lessons. When lessons regularly provide the student with the means and skills to make music she loves and connects with her world, she will increasingly look forward to learning new and more challenging music.

For example, I could play the three-note game "Icha Backa Soda Cracker" with my five-year-old student Audrey for the entire lesson, and she would not get tired of it. In this game, while one of us plays and sings the words, the other taps on some figurines, each time removing the one tapped at the end of the song, until there is only one figurine left. The song is great for technical development, learning about keeping a steady beat, and of course, mastering those three notes. If I were to try that same song with an older beginner, however, the lesson would not only be uninteresting (though technically advantageous), it would likely do serious harm to his motivation and his trust in me as a teacher who shares his love of music.

Another way that music can become more important to our students is to choose music that has powerful significance in their lives. This is why we ask all parents attending our music school about their cultural background or other musical interests. I had one student who wanted to learn nothing but Portuguese "Fado" music — of which I was mostly ignorant — because he visited his grandmother in Portugal every summer. Many students enjoy playing the music they sing at church — from hymns to gospel.

What does this say about technical exercises, especially the dreaded "scales?" There are many teachers today who do not require any "technique" practice whatsoever, while others demand hours of scales, exercises, and boring études. As one of my neighbors (whose children had never attended our music school) recently posted on our neighborhood association Facebook page regarding why he chose to seek out a different music school than ours, "Kids don't want to play scales these days, they want music to be fun!" Personally, I'm not sure this comment is only relevant to kids *"these days."* Many great musicians are on record expressing how much they hated playing scales and exercises. As a teen, I read a quote from my idol, Andrés Segovia, stating that he practiced two hours of scales every day. I tried for years to emulate this but simply could not bring myself to get past 30 minutes before sheer boredom overcame me.

I do, however, ask every one of my students to focus on technique as a part of every lesson, and for the most part, they do it diligently and effectively (if not always with the same eagerness with which they approach their pieces). There are several factors contributing to their willingness and ability to focus on technique in every practice:

1. ACTIVITIES APPROPRIATE TO THE CHILD'S AGE AND DEVELOPMENT

My younger beginners are playing shorter, easier, and "more fun" technical exercises than older, more mature, and advanced students. For example, to develop dexterity in the fourth finger, my young students often play the *Batman* theme ("Dunnu-nunu-nunu-nunu-dunnu-nunu-nunu-nunu Batman!"). Even those who have never seen the old cartoons are delighted by this activity and will show it off to their friends and family.

2.   UNDERSTANDING THE WHY BEHIND THE ACTIVITY

When you are aware of the specific ways your body relates to the instrument, you are able to express more effectively what is in your mind. When children make that connection, they become more willing to invest the energy needed to improve. For example, if a student has inadequate strength in his fingers to play a particular chord in a piece of music he loves, he is likely to be willing to practice an exercise that builds strength.

3.   CLEAR, ATTAINABLE GOALS

The goal is NOT to perform scales over and over. The goal is to play with fluid, expressive control. This involves correct fingering, excellent technique, and an internal feel for expressing the notes. When this has been achieved by the student's own estimation, they are done with that particular exercise.

4.   GAMES, GAMES, GAMES

Rolling dice to determine how many times to repeat the scale correctly, popping a blueberry into a child's mouth every time she gets it correct, or moving a penny from one side of the music stand to the other can all ease the challenge of what could otherwise be seemingly interminable repetition.

How can you help make musical content more relevant? Talk to the teacher about your child's musical interests and which songs he just can't stop singing at home. Share with the teacher aspects of your culture and forward her various recordings of music your family enjoys at home. She may not be able to incorporate all of it right away, but just knowing about it offers the opportunity.

MUSIC LESSON TO LIFE LESSON
Engage in conversations with your child about how what she is learning in school relates to her real world and her own interests. Lemonade stands and (in my household) "slime" production and sale are a great way to make math and science relevant.

Talk to her teachers about finding books that relate to her personal interests. My daughter is a voracious reader, but she mentioned to me the other day that in six years of public school, not a single teacher has ever asked her what she was reading for pleasure. I think that is a terrible, missed opportunity.

Community

Oftentimes we think of disciplined behavior as being something that is entirely up to the individual and certainly something done in isolation. In his book, *The Talent Code*, Daniel Coyle describes the exact opposite: The incredible dedication required to create great talent is grown in tight-knit communities he calls "Talent Hotbeds." These are places such as Florence from 1440 to 1490, where Michelangelo, Donatello, Botticelli, and Da Vinci all interacted, competed, shared ideas, and inspired one another to greater and greater heights. Genius isn't born, it is grown out of intense work and inspiration. The willingness to do the kind of focused, deep practice required to reach truly impressive heights cannot be sustained in a vacuum. You need a community.

I have had the pleasure to witness this in action at our music school in remarkable fashion over the past several months since we announced we were taking forty students to perform at Carnegie Hall. Not only have the students who signed up to go improved their playing, but all the students around them, who have heard them in classes and at recitals, have increased their dedication and focus as well. It is as though a magic wand was waved over our school, and suddenly the level of playing went up.

Another example of the power of Carnegie Hall is the effect it had on my own teacher, Adam Holzman. From the moment he began lessons with Alberto Blain, he knew he was working toward a Carnegie Hall debut at age 17. This is just what all of Mr. Blain's students did, and it was accepted that Adam would follow in the footsteps of the students before him. This "normalizing" of extreme levels of excellence is a major aspect of "Talent Hotbeds."

If we want our children to really catch fire, it is important not only to provide them with access to great teachers, but also to help them find a community of peers who inspire and motivate them to reach and even expand their potential.

Concerts

As any number of self-help books will tell you, goals are the centerpiece of any disciplined behavior. Without clear, motivating, achievable goals, we cannot know where we are going, nor recognize when we get there. Fortunately, music has many built-in goals that are highly motivating. Number one, of course, is performing in a recital or concert. There are other goals besides performances, however, that may be equally, if not more, motivating, such as learning a favorite piece, making it to first chair, self-expression, or learning to play fast or difficult techniques. But music is an art of communication above all else, and the concert is our venue for sharing our art. To study music without getting to perform is akin to practicing soccer without ever having the opportunity to play a game.

Photo courtesy of Matthew Lemke Productions

The trick is to clearly articulate the goal and make a plan on how to achieve it. I am frequently reminding teachers at my music school that signing a student up for a recital a couple of days ahead of time, even if the student is fully prepared to play (which is unlikely) will do nothing to affect his motivation over a long period of time. On the other hand, if he chooses an exciting and challenging new piece several months in advance, learns a couple of preparatory pieces, masters the necessary techniques, carefully learns, memorizes, and practices performing prior to the recital, not only is he more likely to have a positive performance experience, he will also undergo a period of accelerated growth in all areas.

Let's take a closer look at the process Audrey went through in the previously mentioned experience of learning "Moon River" for her parents' 10th anniversary. After her father suggested she perform this piece, I listened to the song and quickly realized that it had several new notes that Audrey had never learned and would require her to learn to play in a new position on the guitar. Since we had enough time, however, I was able to plan several intermediary pieces that could help her tackle these problems one at a time. The goal of performing this iconic piece in such a meaningful setting gave her the motivation to master the musical and technical concepts required for the piece, thus accelerating her development in a short period of time.

This is why it is so important for the child, the teacher, and the parent to set aside time several times per year to establish and check in on motivational goals. Once the goals are set, it is essential to keep them top of mind. Giving them a special place on the music stand, the refrigerator, or on the mirror where your child brushes her teeth will remind her what she's aiming for. Every day she can note her progress toward her goal, focus her energies more efficiently on what she needs to do, and celebrate her accomplishments when she completes them.

Discipline is remembering our deepest dreams every day.

Communication (The Magic Triangle)

A commitment to clear communication must be the foundation upon which we engage in music lessons. In education, communication between teacher and student, between parent and teacher, and between parent and child is often referred to as "The Magic Triangle," and I can assure you that without it, no magic will occur. Many are the talented, devoted students I've had to let go from my studio or music school because there was no clear communication with the parents. Similarly, I have had to work with many teachers over the years who didn't understand that simply presenting the material to the child was not enough.

Communication between the parent and the teacher is so essential that I would go so far as to say that very few, if any, young children will be successful in music study without it. I have had to let some of my most promising students go over the years because the parents were continuously absent from the lesson and difficult to reach. Without their assistance, it was impossible to do my job. Most of this communication should take place during the lessons (each teacher is different, but I ask the parents of four- to seven-year-olds to sit in for the first couple years, the parents of eight- to twelve-year-olds to check in during the last five minutes, and parents of teenagers to check in from time to time as need be). For the more serious issues, a conference can be scheduled in person or over the phone; for routine communication of simple factual information, email is best (however, I have found email can be highly problematic for more subtle or emotional topics).

Teachers need to know what is going on in their students' lives so that they can make appropriate decisions about how to approach each lesson. In my experience, information about what is going on at home can offer quite a lot of insight regarding a student's unique interests and motivators at any given moment. For example, if the teacher is aware that the student's beloved grandparents will be in town soon to visit, she can utilize that to motivate the student to prepare a special song. Alternatively, information about what music is currently trending or that the student enjoys playing or listening to at home can help inform repertoire choices. On the other hand, when there is difficulty or stress in the child's life, we know we should scale back the lesson material, skip a recital, or cut back on the level of difficulty. I once had a particularly sensitive student burst into tears because he felt bad that he was unprepared for the lesson. When I spoke to his mom, she said they had been moving to a new home, and the guitar was packed and unavailable.

For younger children, the parents' role is frequently to assist their child in communicating important information to the teacher. Children will express all kinds of things at home during the week and then either forget or not want to talk about it during the lesson. It can be difficult to know when to speak for your child, when to encourage her to speak for herself, and when to just stay silent and allow your child to express herself in her own time. Nevertheless, the teacher needs your help to discover important things about what is going on in the child's inner life. A good teacher will do everything he can to gain the child's trust and provide a safe environment for communication, but the parent can assist and speed this process along early in the relationship by artfully encouraging good communication.

It is not only our job to advocate for our children, but also to let the teacher know how things are going for us personally with regard to home practice. Often parents seem to feel that struggles with their child around practice are really between them and the child and should not involve the teacher. They may have been struggling to make practice work for months or even years, and the only time I hear about it is when they call to say they are dropping out. To these parents I often say, "You are paying an expert with years of experience to see you and your child every week! Take advantage of this!"

Teachers, for their part, also need to go out of their way to communicate both short-term and long-term expectations and to listen to parents to see how they can modify these goals to fit each child and family. Frequently, for example, teachers take for granted that parents will know that practice time should grow organically from only a few minutes a day at the beginning to whatever is appropriate based on the goals you have set together. Instead, many parents hear that advanced students are practicing several hours a day and make the mistake of trying to get their five-year-old, who knows only two songs, to play for an hour.

The child's role in communication is to learn, over time, how to express himself effectively and respectfully. Some children, such as my own daughter, are so shy that it is extremely difficult for them to speak up for themselves. Others want to spend every minute of every lesson talking to (or arguing with) the teacher. I believe that a loving lesson environment is one of the best environments for learning the skills of respectful communication that are so essential to success later in life. In my daughter's case, we initially would speak for her ("Mei Yin kept saying how much she wants to play this piece in the upcoming recital"), but soon moved on to prompting her to speak up for herself at the beginning of the lesson and finally to talking with her at home about how she can speak up for what she wants in the lesson.

For very young children, gaining impulse control is part of learning to communicate effectively. It is not uncommon (nor inappropriate) for a frustrated child to blurt out something like, "This is stupid!" or "You're making me mess up!" when struggling to play a passage the way in which a teacher has asked. In order for him to learn how to express his frustration appropriately, like anything else, he has to experience failure and loving redirection. On my best days, when my students lose their temper and lash out with their words, I try to say something like, "Thank you for letting me know how you feel. I want to help you play this piece well, but maybe I haven't been helpful. I'm sorry about that. Let's take a little water break." When things are back on a good footing and everyone is calm, it is important to reset clear guidelines for what respectful speech looks and sounds like and how we can notice when we are becoming frustrated and interrupt that cycle before we say something hurtful or inappropriate. This process may take months or even years, but it is one of the most important skills that can be learned in the music lesson (and one I am still learning from my students), and it is worth every minute of the time we give it.

MUSIC LESSON TO LIFE LESSON
"Communication and trust are the two main ingredients for a successful relationship."

— UNKNOWN

Common Roadblocks

It is easy to focus on the motivation side of things and think that that will inevitably lead to frequent and fruitful practice. No matter how motivated the child is, however, if none of her waking hours are spent near a piano, it is unlikely she will ever learn to play piano. In fact, I am of the opinion that music is so intrinsically enjoyable that if we simply remove all roadblocks to playing, most children will spend enough time practicing to make steady improvement. When I call to discuss the reasons why a family has decided to withdraw from lessons at our music school, it nearly always comes down to one of the following common sources of resistance:

Too Busy

This is the hallmark of our age — too busy for life. I have had four-year-olds tell me that they are too busy to practice. This is a real problem, but not one that I think we can afford to accept as a fact of life. I have students (many of them!) who leave for school at 6 AM and return at 7 PM and still practice 30 minutes between dinner and bedtime. For my own family, we decided to send our daughter to a half-day school so that she could have time to hang out with friends, build a website devoted to her passions (reading, writing, and making videos of friends and slime) and still practice every day. My point is twofold: (1) We have more time than we think if we sit down and write out a schedule, and (2) there are options out there for real change.

Power Struggles

I believe one of the most fundamental needs of all humans is the right to control our own actions. As my nephew likes to say about everything — from tying his shoes to buckling the car seat, "I do it myself!" We need to establish trust between the teacher, the child, and the parent. Power struggles typically come in two flavors: fights over practicing and fights over how the parent should interact during practice (e.g., the child doesn't want help, even though he may need it).

From a wide body of research, the results are clear: Strict and attentive parenting yields the best outcomes. When it comes to practice, our children need to know that we are on their side, we will help them make it fun, but if they want to learn piano, they have to practice piano. If they simply refuse, we have two choices: establish a pattern of giving into unreasonable behavior or setting clear boundaries. This doesn't mean we need to fight with them. It is usually more effective to work with consequences: no screens, no dessert, etc., but also no arguing or debating. Of course, we have to investigate and solve the root cause of the resistance, but sometimes it is simply that the child wants total control of her after-school time. If this is the case and we give in, how do we expect to navigate when she refuses to do her homework, or later, come home at a reasonable hour?

The other type of common power struggle is around receiving feedback from a parent during practice. When a teacher assigns a parent to check up on the child at home, she can inadvertently be setting up a power struggle where the parent is watching the child like a hawk and jumping in when something like his posture slips. We wouldn't enjoy doing our job under constant scrutiny, and neither does our child. Remember that no amount of progress at this moment is worth losing that sense of collaboration: *We are working on this together.* When you find yourself engaging in power struggles, back off and wait until things have cooled down before asking (preferably with the teacher present), "How would you like me to help?"

Distractions

No child will practice effectively if his sibling is playing his favorite video game. My wife used to teach two boys at their home. When one of them was having a lesson, the other would be playing video games. The boy in the lesson would often (while still playing) yell up the stairs, "That's my game! Stop playing it right now!" Creating a completely distraction-free environment is impossible, but even a little attention to this can go a long way in removing the worst distractions.

Disliking the Music Assigned

We each have our taste in music, and who doesn't want to play or hear one's favorite songs? For this reason, many teachers take the approach of letting the student choose the music. The child walks into the lesson, and the teacher says, "What do you want to learn today?" Unfortunately, this has two serious problems: (1) The novice cannot know what she doesn't know, so she cannot choose music that is within her reach, and (2) no teacher can know every song ever written, so he will inevitably have to spend part of the lesson looking up the music, learning it himself, and then trying to teach it in a way simplified enough for the student to manage.

A much better approach, in my opinion, is to have an effective curriculum of some of the best music ever written, arranged in an order that can be mastered by just about any learner and from which students can choose their favorites. In addition, the teacher should have a bevy of repertoire that she can use to supplement her standard teaching pieces and a willingness to work toward a few songs per year that the student chooses (*in advance* — so that the teacher can arrange them outside the lesson). In this way, the child has a voice in choosing all the music and the feeling that he will get to play his favorite pieces of music.

ℰↃ

There are also plenty of other, less common sources of resistance to practice, such as physical pain, not liking your teacher, fear of performing, and unhealthy competition. Children will experience any number of obstacles in their path toward excellence in any field. The important thing is not so much to teach that they must fight through difficulty, but that they can use their own creativity and rely upon the assistance of the adults in their lives to come up with solutions. A wonderful example I heard once, on the radio show *From the Top*, was of a young violinist whose commute to and from school was so lengthy that it interfered with practice time. To give her more time to practice, her parents bought a car with a sunroof so that she could sit in the back and practice without the bow hitting the roof.

In the end, overcoming adversity makes us prouder of our accomplishments, builds self-esteem, and makes us stronger.

10 Tips to Help Children Love Practicing

People often think love of music is something that just "happens" to you. Maybe for some people it is — I just haven't met them. All the student and professional musicians I have ever known can point to many small things that made music special for them and made the hard work of practice easier. Of course, they all say they loved the sound of this singer or that band or this instrument, and from that, it can be easy to conclude that they just "loved music," but your child (if she is struggling to practice willingly) does not. If you drill down and ask these musicians how they got around to practicing, however, it always comes out that there were many factors motivating them to come back to the instrument day after day. I have found it helpful to collect all the positive musical practice experiences I could find from everyone and anyone who would share them: from dozens of books, to interviews with parents and professional musicians, to my own students, to doing surveys. Here are a few that I believe to be the most helpful for the first stage of learning, when our primary goal here is for our children to develop a love of playing and a solid foundation of good habits.

> First of all, take care of the basics: Is your child rested, fed, safe, supported, and happy?

1. *Remove Roadblocks*

Always remember that practicing is challenging and rewarding simultaneously. Like climbing a mountain or running a race, you need to be relaxed, ready, and focused. Before exploring more complex motivational issues, it is important to ensure that we take care of the basics: Are we rested, fed, safe, supported, and happy? Is there enough time to ease into our practice with curiosity and love, or does it have to be squeezed into the only five-minute block between homework and bed?

With today's busy schedules, simply getting home with enough time to eat and get to bed can be a challenge. Often a parent will come to me and say, "I just don't think music is for Suzy. Whenever I ask her to go the piano, she whines and cries." My usual response is just to ask him to describe a typical day leading up to practice. Quite often by the time the parent is finished describing their day, he has a very different explanation for why Suzy doesn't want to practice. A typical response might be, "Well, we're up at 6:30, so I can drop her off on my way to work, and I pick her up at 5:30 on my way home. On Tuesdays and Thursdays, we grab a bite to eat on our way to swimming from 6:00 to 7:00, and on Wednesdays we do Kumon. By the time we get home, we're both exhausted. We have plenty of time on Monday, Friday, and the weekends — except when we go out of town or have family visiting. Hmmm. I guess that isn't much time after all." Imagine the piano lesson is on Monday and there is no time to practice until Friday; how likely is it that the child (or parent) will have a clear memory of excitement for the new songs, clear practice steps, and muscle memory of where the fingers go?

2. Make a Schedule

If you were to ask most kids, "Would it be easier to practice once a week or once a day?" they would say, "Once a week." They would be wrong, however. In my experience, it is much easier to get children to do something that is part of a daily routine than something that is less predictably part of their lives. This is partly because they become used to it, but also because they become good at it. Daily practice may be a struggle at first, but if at the beginning we make efforts to make it fun and rewarding to overcome their natural resistance to changing their routine, pretty soon they can play some really fun music and start to enjoy it, especially if they get to perform for an appreciative audience at the end of the practice.

Making a plan is, of course, one of the most basic steps toward achieving any goal. With music practice, this usually means a practice schedule. For some families, life is pretty regulated and predictable, with a fairly uniform routine Monday to Friday and a different routine on the weekends. For others, every week is a new adventure, with sports, travel, playdates, and more occurring at completely different times each week. Most of us, of course, are somewhere in between. In my experience, however, whether your life is predictable or not, making a schedule results in greater peace of mind, higher levels of achievement, and less conflict. The only difference between the two extremes is how often you remake the schedule. Some families may be able to make one schedule that works for months; others may need to make a new schedule every day. Either way, here are some things to consider when building an effective schedule:

- Be reasonable and take personal needs into account.
- Leave some wiggle room.
- Don't freak out if you miss something on your list.
- Less is more: A schedule is like a budget — you have only so much time to spend, so spend it wisely.

3. *Make It Fun!*

It is entirely possible that your child may find practicing his instrument to be the most fun part of his day. In that case, hurrah for you! However, if this is not the case (or if it was, but that has changed), please know that this is completely normal and that there are millions of parents like you, many of whom (often with the aid of their children's teachers) have come up with a variety of easy-to-implement ways of making practice fun. Here are just a few tricks parents have used to bring joy to the practice room:

- Toss a piece of popcorn into her mouth every time she plays a phrase correctly.
- Move a penny from one side of the music stand to the other every time she plays a phrase correctly.
- Have a "Dance-Off" where you dance to her pieces, and she rates your interpretation (this was my daughter's favorite). If you can play, you can each have an interpretive dance competition while the other plays — or have the stuffed animals compete!

For more ideas, see the section "10 Games You Can Play with Your Child" on pages 61–63.

4. *Make a Happy Place*

If the space in which you practice feels warm and inviting, is filled with objects that make you smile, is distraction-free, and is, basically, your favorite place in the house — who wouldn't want to be there?

Of course, it is essential that your child be in on this process, but he needs parental guidance to make the right choices. My daughter tried practicing with her puppy in her lap, but obviously that didn't last very long. My daughter often had her stuffed animals surrounding her when she practiced. We put up trophies she had earned through her music practice and pictures of her concerts.

Conversely, a lonely, distracting, or unpleasant environment can make progress difficult and create an unnecessary resistance to practice. Taking time to decorate the area in a way that inspires, promotes focus, and allows for a good set-up on the instrument is well worth the time. It can take a while, however, to really notice what is working for him and what is working against him.

5. Make a Joyful Routine

Developing discipline is about learning about ourselves and what works for us to stay motivated about reaching our goals. If you are so motivated that you can practice in a cold, noisy room with someone leaning over your shoulder criticizing you, then I say, "More power to you." For myself, however, I prefer to have a nice cup of hot tea or coffee, to lotion my hands then soak them in warm water, and to start by running through one of my favorite pieces or improvising a little song for myself. That way, when I think about all I have to do each day, practice seems like the oasis of calm in the middle of a hectic rat-race. I look forward to it as "my time."

For kids, creating an effective routine that works for them is not something that comes naturally (for the most part). The most common routine children have in my experience is usually some variation of this: Johnny walks in the door, grabs a cookie (gets yelled at), and opens the iPad to play Minecraft. Plays until his mom notices and says, "Get on the piano right now! We have to take your brother to baseball in 15 minutes, and your teacher will kill you if you go another week without practice."

Johnny resentfully bangs through his pieces as fast as he can and somehow finishes with enough time to get back on the iPad. As they rush out the door, his mom says, "I thought I told you to practice?!!!"

Johnny yells back, "I did!" and off they go.

Perhaps I exaggerate a little here, but honestly, I have heard similar stories dozens of times. Usually followed by, "I don't know what happened. He was so excited to start piano; I guess he just lost interest."

The truth is that a child can love music deeply and still be attracted to Minecraft after a long day at school. It is our job to help our kids learn that screens are not an effective means of letting our minds unwind and rejuvenate when we are tired. Research (and the experience of every parent always) shows that using a screen keeps the brain out of its regenerative state. We all know our children are more grumpy, unfocused, and unmotivated to learn when they put down their computer games, so why do we allow them to get on in the first place? The answer is simply that it is easier that way — at least in the moment, though not in the long run.

Even if your child is completely screen-free, there may be aspects of the ritual around practice that aren't serving you or her. My suggestion is to take some time to create a joyful routine that works for your whole family. Be thoughtful about meeting needs for food, rest, and personal time. Try to keep the routine simple, and don't let it take too long (part of my daughter's routine when she was younger was setting up her stuffed animals, but she could take 45 minutes doing this, so we had to make some adjustments). The goal is to have something to look forward to and to develop a pattern that allows the brain to settle into a positive learning state of mind.

6. *Parent Present or Not?*

Deciding whether or not to sit with your child during each and every practice is an important and difficult decision. We want to help them love their practice, but if our presence leads to conflict and negativity, then it isn't helpful. In the initial stages of lessons, especially for very young children, it may be necessary to have a parent at least get them started, simply because they cannot read or remember what the teacher said to practice. Fortunately, most children of this age actually prefer a parent to work with them.

From about the ages of four to seven, my daughter wanted one of us to be present and, often, interacting with her during the practice. If we were busy and asked her to practice alone, it was as though we had condemned her to the gallows. As she got older, she just wanted to know we were nearby, and so I would often just sit on the couch and read. Now she prefers us to be out of the house most of the time when she practices (probably because I can't always keep my mouth shut about her practice habits).

Many parents report that they would like to sit with their child during practice, and their child loves it when they do so, but they simply don't have the time between getting home from work, getting another child to sports practice, getting dinner on the table, helping with homework, etc. In this case, it usually works out to help them get set up, go over what they need to practice, and give them some fun way of tracking their progress (like popcorn or pennies!). If they complete everything, they can have a reward such as giving a concert of their favorite piece before bed.

7. Start with Their Favorite Piece

I see a lot of teachers write scales and technical drills at the top of their students' practice goals. I completely understand the desire to settle into the basics of technique, warm up the fingers, and become aware of our bodies through technique, and I absolutely do this myself and have my more advanced students do this as well. For young students, however, our primary goal is to instill a love of music and playing. Assigning the most boring parts of playing right at the beginning of practice is like saying, "Eat your broccoli first" when calling them to the dinner table. I know most of us parents tell our children they have to eat their vegetables if they want their dessert, but fortunately in music practice there is nothing that we do that is "unhealthy," so we can start with our favorite part of music practice every time! Allowing our students and children to choose what to play first is also a great way to allow them to feel in control of the situation, which is vital to their developing ownership of the learning process and gradually becoming aware of their own personalized discipline (i.e., what works for them). For some students, this may be improvising (or "just messing around" as many parents call it). For others, it may be music from a favorite movie or show. Some actually enjoy their technical work because it fascinates them. Whatever is most attractive to them is a great entryway into enjoying practice. At the moment, my own daughter always wants to save the best for last in all things (musical or not). That's fine too. Whatever works.

8. *Don't Push — Attract*

It is natural for anyone to push back against anything they are being pushed into. If we say, "Playing Minecraft is something you can do only once all your chores, homework, and practice are done," then we have set up a dynamic in which practice (like chores and homework) are, at best, things to be tolerated or avoided, and Minecraft is the goal or reward.

If, on the other hand, we can find a way to make practice (even for a short period of time) an enjoyable activity, then we can use this trick to turn the tables:

Tell your child they are practicing too much, and you think they need more time to "just have fun." Set a timer for ten minutes, and the student MUST stop after ten minutes. Perhaps we can find creative ways that they can earn more practice time (for example, if they really want to practice more, then if they are super focused for the first ten minutes, they can earn an extra five).

WARNING: This only works if you have *first* established practice as an enjoyable activity.

This approach has two benefits: One, they need to decide how to make maximum use of their time. Rather than simply playing through their old favorites over and over, they may decide, "Well, if I only have ten minutes, let me learn that new section of my new song right now!" The other benefit is that they might try to sneak in extra practice here and there.

This is what my practice was like every day as a kid. My parents always had more chores for me, and when I practiced at night, they complained that I kept them awake. I was always trying to sneak away to play guitar, and they were always trying to get me to do something more useful.

9. *Better to Do a Little Than Nothing at All*

We often feel stressed or that there isn't enough time to do anything. In those moments, we should remind ourselves (and, by extension, our children) that it is always better to do a little bit than nothing at all. Not to say that you should rush through all your pieces in two minutes because you have to get to your baseball practice or math pentathlon or whatever. Just take a breath and see if there is something you can accomplish in the time you have.

Often taking the time to do a little something will be the spark we need to light our fire for later in the day or the next day when we have an unexpected bit of free time!

10. *No Screen Time till Practice and Homework Are Done*
In a survey of over one hundred parents at our music school, the number one most commonly recommended tip for getting kids to practice was (not surprisingly) "No screen time until you're done." We have had parents say, "Oh, I never have to remind them to practice — they run to the piano, then get their homework done because they know all screens are off limits until they get their work done."

Personally, I have mixed feelings about music being primarily a form of "work" for which screen time is a "reward," but personalized discipline is about whatever works for your unique family. With my daughter (and myself), we limited screen time more than most families would (I didn't even get a TV or a cell phone until 2017 because I feared the distraction they would cause).

I *do* think it is extremely helpful to analyze what activities bring us value. When we notice our kids are more grumpy, distracted, and unhappy after a particular activity, it is probably wise to begin a discussion in the family about doing that less. When we notice they are happy, proud, or satisfied with another activity, no matter how much they may resist it at the beginning, we can find ways to increase that activity. For younger children, it may be a matter of skillfully redirecting them to the healthier behaviors. With older children, we need to engage them in conversations about becoming their best selves so that they can begin to discern how to make healthy choices for themselves.

A Word on Rewards

Rewards for practice is a controversial subject. Performing well for an appreciative audience is the most wonderful feeling in the world, and accordingly, some teachers and parents think that anything else could potentially stunt our intrinsic motivation. There is some limited research that indicates that this is possible. In very limited situations, giving rewards for a period of time to kids for activities they already enjoy doing and then removing rewards suddenly results in children engaging in the activity less than before the rewards were introduced.

That being said, there are many ways to use rewards that have been shown to have a positive effect and are easily stepped away from once the child has outgrown that motivational system. Remember, rewards are best when:

- Motivation isn't enough to overcome resistance, and we have done all we can think of to reduce the things that are getting in the way of practice.
- Rewards are given out based on thoughtful, objective reflection by the learner ("Did you accomplish the goals set by the teacher?" "Yes, I played each phrase slowly three times before performing it for my stuffed animals.")
- Rewards are unpredictable with regard to when and how much. Just as gambling is only interesting (and even addictive) because we can never be sure when or if we will get the prize, reward systems are vastly more effective when they are unpredictable. This also avoids the child making a value assessment and deciding that frozen blueberries just aren't worth 15 minutes of practice.
- Rewards are small enough not to become more important than the activity itself. Particularly effective are rewards of attention (going to the exotic pet shop was a major motivator for one of our students for several years) or rewards related to music that they love, such as going to a concert. By contrast, "If you practice every day for a month, I will buy you a new phone," is likely to focus a child's attention on the phone rather than on the skills she is developing (though I have seen this exact bribe work just fine). Ultimately, you will know what works best for your own family.

Emergency Rescue Tips!

Occasionally I have parents come to me asking for suggestions on how to recover from a contentious and negative practice environment. Have no fear: One child who cut the strings on his guitar because he so desperately wanted to quit went on to become a professional guitarist! It is possible to recover from a bad relationship with music. Every situation is unique, but here are a few tips.

- First, discover the source or sources of the negativity. Check what we've discussed here: Is it a power struggle? Then back off and give some choice to the child. Is it a roadblock? Then make sure the basics are in place (time, nutrition, mindset, etc.). Is it the music? Then change what songs he is learning
- Establish trust that you will solve this together. You can say, "I know that playing music isn't fun right now, but we can make it something you love to do if we work together."
- Establish a routine you can both agree upon and stick to it.
- Create a reward system based upon the child's own evaluation of the quality of her work. If she can tell you what she did that was good, then she will reflect upon that and incorporate it into her behavior more in the future.
- Talk to the teacher about turning things around through any means possible: changing music, changing performance goals, working with other students — anything! If the teacher is inflexible, it may be time to think about changing teachers.

The Three Levels of Motivation

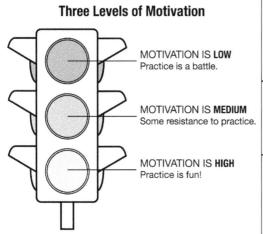

Three Levels of Motivation

MOTIVATION IS **LOW**
Practice is a battle.

MOTIVATION IS **MEDIUM**
Some resistance to practice.

MOTIVATION IS **HIGH**
Practice is fun!

What to Do at Each Level
GET CREATIVE FAST! • Try something new • Communicate with teacher and child • Use a reward system • Remove roadblocks
NORMAL, BUT TRY TWEAKING • Catch them succeeding • Sign up for an exciting goal • Check in regularly
USE THIS TIME TO BUILD SKILLS • Take on a big challenge • Improve a weakness • Build connections • Notice what's working and keep doing it!

When practice is a struggle, parents often see it as a sign that music isn't the right activity for their child, rather than the perfect opportunity to learn about how to be motivated toward something difficult. Similarly, when practice is fun and easy, parents may take it for granted that "at least this is one thing we don't have to worry about." The only time everyone seems appropriately engaged is when things are just bumping along — not great, but not a disaster either.

I would like to propose that each level of motivation is an opportunity to learn more about ourselves and what works best for us: When we are on fire, use that fire to build amazing skills that will lead to self-confidence and increased love of music. When we are doing just okay, we can celebrate the successes and have the time to adjust what's not working, so long as we stay in communication. When practice is a struggle, that's the time to grow into the person we truly want to become: skillful at overcoming challenges, gritty, and creative.

6

STAGE TWO:
DEVELOPING DISCIPLINE

"My parents used to always say, 'All we wanted was to teach our kids discipline through music, and we got two professional guitarists out of the deal.'"
– ADAM HOLZMAN, CONCERT GUITARIST

When children begin music lessons at a young age (eight or younger), their ability to set long-term goals, engage in effective time management, break complex tasks down into small parts, etc., is generally not very well developed. This is, of course, natural and appropriate. We *want* our kids to be kids — to live in the moment and to enjoy and experience everything now as fully as possible without worrying about the future. Early on, disciplined behavior (as well as determining how much "fun" and how much focus on skill development is appropriate) is mostly determined by the parents and teachers in the child's life. More importantly, it is our job to gradually teach him the skills needed to become self-reliant, self-motivated, and capable of setting and achieving his own goals.

Taking a gradual approach to developing discipline in children is one of the most under-researched and difficult

Photo courtesy of Marina Peterson

processes facing parents and teachers. There are hundreds of books such as Gladwell's *Outliers*, Coyle's *The Talent Code*, and Ericsson's *Peak* describing exactly how disciplined people behave. There are many parenting books that help us create a joyful and loving environment for our children. But there are few that describe how to help children move gradually from a joyful, but somewhat casual relationship with a subject to becoming children who practice with focus and determination and who can achieve anything to which they set their minds.

Some parents believe that if a child loves something enough, she will devote the time and energy needed to achieve excellence in that area — essentially that discipline is an expression of level of interest. In my experience, you have to have a love for what you do, but that is not enough, in and of itself, to cause you to develop all the skills needed to achieve excellence. You have to learn an entirely different set of abilities — time management, problem-solving, goal setting, etc. — in order to develop the skills involved in your area of interest. This is great news because it is these skills that are most valuable in achieving other aspirations in life!

So how do we teach our children and our students to become "self-disciplined?" How do we go from a playful, joyful approach to life to one in which we are able to set goals, reach them, and feel proud of our achievements (while still maintaining a joyful outlook)? The answer, I believe, is SLOWLY. One step at a time, one discussion at a time, one small task at a time, we gradually give responsibility over to our children. This is why each chapter contains practical tips on practicing for each stage of development. Pick one thing to try out, give it a couple weeks, and if it isn't working, try something else.

Great teaching and parenting involve understanding the child, giving her manageable, growth-oriented tasks, then reflecting on and gradually improving the outcomes.

The assistance of an experienced teacher or coach can be extremely helpful in this transition from joyful playing to serious practicing. Someone who has been through the process multiple times with different children and different families can suggest when it might be time to allow the student to choose how many days a week to practice, in which recitals (if any) he would like to perform, and whether he needs to focus on technique, repertoire, or music theory this practice session.

Most parents fall into one of two opposite traps in the process of giving responsibility to their child: Either they keep everything the same for too long (and who can blame them — it worked last year!), or they shift the responsibility all at once (usually because they are sick of the power struggle).

Pianist Hilda Huang suggests, "By age 10 or 11, the child needs to learn that what you put in is what you get out. What your parents put in, *you* don't get out." Assuming the child started young, this is entirely possible, but how do we get there from here? Just because someone "needs to learn" something, doesn't mean that she *will* learn that thing. Great teaching and parenting involve understanding the child, giving her tasks she can manage and from which she can learn, and then reflecting on and gradually improving upon the outcomes. The purpose of this book is to help you develop those teaching skills so that you may effectively teach your child to love practice and develop discipline over a long period of time.

First let us consider what conditions must exist for them to be ready to begin developing discipline through music.

Markers of Stage-Two Readiness: Love, Habits, and No Roadblocks

Every time I teach a workshop on discipline, parents ask me, "How long until they can begin practicing on their own?" The answer, of course, depends on the child and the experiences he has had up to that point. Rather than asking, "How long?" we should ask, "Is he ready?"

> If we want our children to be successful, the best approach is to provide the conditions for success and *teach* them how to be successful.

Ideally, once a child has been playing music for a while (for some children, it will be several years, for others it will be several months, depending largely on how old they were when they began), his skill on the instrument will allow him to play several pieces of music confidently and with ease and will therefore garner admiration from family and peers. Because he loves the sound of his own playing and does so with considerable ease for his best pieces, he is able to lose himself in a state of "Flow" and reach a joyful state of mind through music. Because he recognizes the time and effort he has put in to achieve this skill, he is justifiably proud, and his self-esteem is well established. If this is the case, beginning conversations about setting goals that are in line with his own passion will be quite easy. Not that a young child will likely choose music over video games and playing with friends, but he will understand that if he wants to take his playing to the next level and perform on a special concert or talent show (or any other goal he chooses), then he must be willing to commit to a greater sacrifice of time.

Unfortunately, the more common path for young children consists of the teacher choosing music that is uninteresting to the student and the parents forcing their child to practice (albeit somewhat erratically because of their busy schedule). As a result, the child cannot play anything exceptionally well, associates the instrument with forced servitude, and does not enjoy music. It is at this point that parents often decide it is time for their child to take some responsibility for her practice. They (the parents) are sick and tired of fighting over practice, and if Misha doesn't want to practice, then she should just quit. Alternatively, the parents may take the unreasonable position in which they won't let her quit, but she now has to practice on her own. This is the equivalent of saying, "I have driven you to school for ten years now. It is time for you to drive yourself." Not only does the child lack the skills to practice on her own, but she also lacks the motivation.

If we want our children to be successful, the best approach is to provide the conditions for success and then *teach* them how to be successful. Expectations of success can be helpful, but expectations are not, in and of themselves, a sufficient condition for learning.

Accordingly, before you begin handing over responsibility for practice, you should ask yourself these three questions:

- "Does he love the music he plays?"
- "Have we established a good habit of practice?"
- "Have we eliminated obvious roadblocks to practice?"

If you answered "yes" to each of these questions, then you can begin teaching the principles of personalized discipline to your child and expect a high level of success. If the answer is "no," then it will be fruitless to attempt to move forward. The only way forward is to go back to develop Stage One ("Loving Practice and Establishing Habits"). Please see "Emergency Rescue Tips" on page 96.

Evolving Conversations around Discipline

We all live busy lives and, for most of us, maintaining a constant awareness of our child's developmental progress toward independent discipline is decidedly *not* on the schedule. The alternatives, however, are either the disappointment of giving up or a never-ending struggle of forcing her to follow our rules. Either way, she will not learn to take responsibility for achieving the goals she set for herself until much later (if ever).

Furthermore, having these conversations about discipline regularly over a period of years can help us reduce the stress of an over-scheduled life, filled with hurry, conflict, and disappointment. Committing to engaging in this process slowly is like building a dam to protect our village from floods: It is hard to do when you are already flooded, but once it is done, you will flood much less often! A hurricane of unexpected events may still overwhelm your family, but, unlike a real dam, the skills of discipline will actually be strengthened every time we use them successfully to navigate a severe challenge.

It is tempting to want to accomplish this growth toward independence in a single conversation or two: "It is time you took some responsibility for your own practice. What schedule would you like to set for yourself?" Done. Unfortunately, this is not how most children grow and learn. A radical change in the way we manage our schedules and approach challenges will need to be handled slowly and gradually so that they can experience increasingly positive results, associate those rewards with their disciplined choices, and therefore increase their willingness to take on even more difficult challenges effectively.

The qualities of these conversations are the same as the qualities of any good conversation. They will involve genuine interest from both parties, curiosity in what each other has to say, willingness to respect and try each other's suggestions, and a sense of collaboration toward a mutually beneficial outcome. If your child perceives these conversations as lectures (as my daughter, very reasonably, often did), then it is likely you need to adopt a tone of greater curiosity, willingness to listen, and less attachment to controlling the outcome of the conversation. Nobody wants to talk to someone who has already determined what should be said. The classic lecture followed by, "I'm glad we had this little talk, and both agree that things are going to change around here" isn't going to help anyone.

In Stage One we, the parents and teachers, take responsibility for increasing motivation and reducing resistance; we help build a positive mindset through the words we use to praise; and we build grit by saying, "We're sticking with this, *and* together we will find a creative way to make it fun!" When children are ready to begin Stage Two, we simply change our mindset from managing the situation to bringing our children and students into the conversation. In addition to creating motivation by choosing music they will enjoy or a practice time that works for them, we bring them into the conversation to choose wisely among several positive options. Gradually, as they become more practiced at making good decisions and noticing the positive results of those decisions, we give them more and more control over the process until, eventually, they are doing most of the heavy lifting and we are simply there on the sidelines cheering for them.

Why not go straight to letting our kids make their own decisions, experience the consequences, and learn from them? It all comes back to readiness and experience. Let us use the process of choosing when, what instrument, and what teacher as a stand-in for all the possible conversations around developing discipline. Many parents bring their three- or even two-year-old child to my school saying, "My daughter wants to learn violin, and I think it is important to respect her interest and start when she is asking to start. We want to meet several teachers, and the one she connects with the best is the one we will choose." A two-year-old wanting to play violin, however, has no way of knowing the challenges that simply holding a violin will entail, let alone setting her fingers on the right spot and drawing a bow across the strings. She will likely be attracted to the nicest teacher, and, while kindness is an essential trait in teachers, so is good training, a solid curriculum, and a plan for success.

> Until children have experience with success, they have no basis for making successful decisions.

It is unreasonable to expect children of any age (or adults for that matter) to know much of anything about something they have never encountered, especially something as complicated as the development of musical skill. We can extend this idea to every aspect of the decision-making process: when, how long, what songs to learn, performances or not, etc. Until they have experience with success, they have no basis for making successful decisions.

Steps to Self-Discipline Conversations

Notice	Ask Questions	Listen & Support	Self-Evaluation
Catch successes! Brag on them!	Encourage conversation about practice.	Be positive!	Let's try this and see what happens.
1	2	3	4

Step One: Noticing

By tapping into what might have made a certain practice or lesson particularly fun and productive, we are already beginning to lay the groundwork for meaningful conversations in Stage One. If we make a point of "catching our kids succeeding" rather than catching them failing, we increase the positive interactions around practice and reinforce the behaviors we want to see. One trick a therapist once shared with me that she uses on her child is to brag to her spouse in front of her child about the behaviors she wants to reinforce. "Whoa. You will never believe what Kara did today after school." Even when our kids know we are doing this on purpose, my experience is that they love the attention and love that we noticed and shared.

Of course, we have to set up an environment in which productive behaviors are likely to occur if we want to catch them at those behaviors. If you want to catch your child practicing on his own without being reminded, you will need to be at home at the same time as your child, without the TV or Internet distracting him. If you want him to practice for longer periods of time, he will need enough music and exercises to make practice last longer.

What those conversations might look like:

Motivation/Resistance — "I noticed you smiling a lot during practice this morning. It looked like you were enjoying yourself more than when we tried to practice right before bed."

Mindset — "Wow! You worked on that section for a really long time, and it is really sounding great! Great job!"

Grit — "I am so proud of you for sticking with this. I know it's hard, but that's something I've noticed about you — you don't shy away from a challenge."

Effective Practice — "You slowed down and played that hard spot several times before speeding it up again. I've heard that's a great practice habit that only top musicians use!"

Step Two: Asking Questions

Frequently simply opening the conversation with a positive observation (so long as it is honest) will elicit a response that leads to a productive conversation. When I compliment my daughter for her hard work or focused practice, she usually just gives me a big smile and looks contented. From time to time, however, she will reveal something useful like, "I don't like practicing after school because I know my friends are all playing, and I want to join them." If the child volunteers such information, great! If not, we can encourage the conversation by asking questions. Some that have worked for me:

Motivation/Resistance — "I noticed you practiced a lot longer today and didn't seem to get tired. I actually had to STOP you from practicing to come to dinner. What do you think was making you want to play longer?"

Mindset — "I noticed you took the time to carefully go through your teacher's suggestions before you started. What made you approach the music differently today?"

Grit — "I noticed that even though a lot of your friends have quit piano, you are sticking with it. What makes you want to keep going after all these years?"

Effective Practice — "What do you think the best way to tackle your new piece would be?"

Step Three: Listening and Supporting

It should be obvious that if we ask a question we should listen intently to the answer, but I can tell you that for myself, I've come to realize I have a subconscious habit of listening only to the answers I want to hear. If we cannot muster a sense of true curiosity about what our child is telling us, it is unlikely he will want to continue sharing.

Motivation/Resistance — If we hear something like, "I like it when you are in the kitchen and don't tell me what to do!" it can be easy to feel defensive and respond with something like, "I'm only trying to help. You know you play your pieces too fast!" But this is likely just to reignite old power struggles. Instead, we can support her observation and, at the same time, ask if there is any way she would like our help. "I can understand that, and I certainly enjoy hearing you play while I'm cooking. I don't like it when my boss hovers over me while I'm at work either. Is there any other way you would like me to help you be aware of what areas your teacher wanted you to improve this week?"

Mindset — If we hear, "This piece is really hard, but it's fun to figure out how the notes fit together," we can respond with, "That's a great way to approach challenges! Maybe you are ready for harder pieces like this. Do you think we should ask your teacher for more pieces like this one?"

Grit — If we hear, "I like to stick with things because I know I am getting better every day, and I want to play like Elton John," we can respond with, "I'm sure Elton John played for thousands of hours before he wrote his first hit song. You are on your way, and you are right: I hear you getting better every day!"

Effective Practice — If we hear, "This part is really hard! I can't do it," most of us might respond with, "Yes you can! Just keep trying!" An alternative would be to say, "Yeah, that does sound hard. Let's see what your teacher wrote, or maybe we can send him an email about it!" (Personally, I tell every student that I would rather take five minutes during the week to answer an email than thirty minutes during the lesson to fix a bad habit.) The more important fact here is that *our child has recognized a difficult spot and is seeking solutions, which is infinitely better than simply ignoring the problem!* We need to listen and support his request for assistance, and while it can be good to say, "Let's take a look at it, and see what we can do before we give up," it is fine to reach out for help — that is a disciplined behavior too!

Step Four: Experimenting Leads to Self-Evaluation

Self-evaluation is one of the most important skills demonstrated by successful learners. The ability to try things one way, evaluate the relative success or failure, and make a course adjustment is the difference between giving up when we encounter

> *"Success is moving from failure to failure without the loss of enthusiasm."*
> — **Anonymous**

adversity and continuing to grow and improve. After all, as someone once said, "Success is moving from failure to failure without the loss of enthusiasm." In my experience, asking my students to evaluate the success of different practice strategies is more effective once they have experienced several successful strategies and expressed how they felt or why they chose to practice that way. Only once they have noticed the results of good practice will they be in a position to evaluate their own practice.

When I was first trying this with my daughter, my attempts were so clumsy that they always came across as thinly-disguised criticism (which, in fact, they were).

Me: What did you think of that practice?
Mei Yin: Um … good?
Me: Good?!
Mei Yin (dejectedly): I guess I could have taken more time on the hard spots …

This was decidedly *not* a conversation and definitely did not add to her motivation to be a better musician.

As time went on and I made an effort to really listen, I found that conversations happened more easily when they were set up ahead of time. For example, I might suggest trying to practice two different ways (say, before school and after school), and we could talk about how each one worked for us. When she was anticipating the conversation, there was no sense of surprise and no suspicion of an ulterior motive. I was curious about her input, and she was interested in my feedback.

Setting up conversations with "Let's try this and see how it goes" is at the essence of personalized discipline. Not just for our kids, but for ourselves as well. Finding out what works for each of us is only possible if we try different approaches, evaluate, and make adjustments.

If we have been discussing motivation, mindset, and grit regularly in our household, we can set up the conversations to reflect how our behaviors impact those areas of our lives. For example:

- "I notice you are tired and grumpy when we try to practice right before bed. Let's try a couple different times to practice and see which one feels the happiest."
- "Let's try a couple different ways to increase motivation this semester and see which ones have the most impact."

Checking Our State of Mind Before Starting Conversations

If both parents and children are aware of their past successes and then enter into conversations about motivation, mindset, grit, and practice with an open mind and a curiosity about discovering new ways to learn and grow, we can be fairly certain to have a productive, or at least, relaxed and enjoyable conversation. However, the perfect environment is not a necessary precondition for beginning conversation. There is no one "right" way to have a conversation; if there were, it really wouldn't be conversation. Nevertheless, it is worthwhile to note that if any of the parties involved are upset or angry or hungry, then problem-solving is highly unlikely.

So long as we are noticing our own internal state when we are speaking and noticing the impact of our words, we are likely to be able to make adjustments as we go to improve the quality of both our child's practice and our time together. I still regularly catch myself wanting to tell my daughter what she is doing wrong and how to practice better; if I have the ability to notice my own feelings at those times, I often notice that I am experiencing unrelated unpleasant feelings and really wanting more control in other areas of my life. Conversations that begin while I am in that state of mind rarely improve our relationship or her practice. When I fall short of my goals for myself (which is common), I try to make a point of not waiting too long before I apologize. "I'm so sorry I interfered with your practice unasked. I am angry about something that was said at work, but that is no excuse for not respecting your space. I hope you can forgive me." We don't have to be perfect for this process to work — in fact, falling short, apologizing, and trying a new approach is a model for the behavior we want to see.

MUSIC LESSON TO LIFE LESSON
Demonstrating our own ability to notice our successes and failures as parents and make adjustments as we go will greatly help our children learn to notice the relative levels of success and failure in their efforts on their instruments and apply those to their schoolwork, friendships, and chores.

Joining a Community to Build Discipline

The best thing I have found to help my students remain focused on learning, working hard to develop grit, and using their best practice tools is to get them engaged in new and interesting projects. The best projects are ones they choose themselves and ones that involve their peers. The excitement of working together on a shared goal super-charges motivation and releases the energy required for significant improvement.

Over the years, I have seen this level of engagement when I took students to perform at Carnegie Hall in New York, when a guitar trio chose to travel across the state to compete, and when my daughter composed a piece of music for a trio of friends, which they later performed together.

One of the most imaginative projects I have seen is something my wife, Wendy, is doing with eight of her students this year called the One Hundred Piece Challenge. Based on an idea from Elissa Milne's "The More You Learn, the More You Know" in *Clavier Companion* magazine, at the beginning of the year Wendy challenged her intermediate students to master one hundred pieces this year. First, she asked them each to come up with descriptions of what would qualify as mastery, and she put their answers together to form a standard for excellence. Then she purchased a magnet board and some small dry-erase magnets upon which they could write the names of the pieces they had mastered as they completed them. She had the students pick photos that they felt described their pieces. Finally, she set a date for a concert in which they would perform their pieces, while the chosen photos were projected on a screen overhead.

The beauty of a project such as this is that the traditional do-what-the-teacher-says style of learning is turned completely on its head. The students set the standards; the students evaluate if they have met them. The students explore the world through music and images and can celebrate their progress at the end. Wendy has said that this year she hardly needed to teach at all. Her job was simply to help her students pick pieces at the appropriate level of challenge, help them with problem-solving when they hit a roadblock, and ensure they were still developing in the areas of sight-reading, theory, and technique. When it came to curiosity and a willingness to work hard, the magnet board took care of that. Every day the students walked in the room, they would check the board to see how many magnets their friends had put up and look forward to adding their own. If their pieces didn't measure up to their own standards, they would typically say, "I'm going to work twice as hard this week so I can put up two pieces next week!" (This, of course, was not only an example of a learner's mindset, but of grit.)

Co-Creating Habits of Discipline

In Stage One of developing discipline, we, the parents and teachers, take responsibility for creating joyful lesson and practice experiences. In Stage Two, we enter the same process, but this time with the equal collaboration of our child. Where before *we* created a routine we knew worked

> *"Discipline is not the ability to sit in front of a doughnut and not eat it. It is the choice to not sit in front of doughnuts."*
> — **Unknown**

well with their meals, play, sleep, and school schedules (as well as our own), we now talk to them about what might work and co-create a new routine together. We establish the expectation ahead of time that everything new will be tested to see if it is working — and adjusted if it is not.

In fact, every aspect of joyful and effective practice that we put into place in Stage One (including, but not limited to, what music they're learning, whether or not we sit with them during practice, what kind and how many performances, how much and how frequently they practice, and even the instrument and the teacher with whom they study) becomes much more of a collaborative decision. Whereas previously we limited their choices to a few options we knew would work for them, in Stage Two we begin a conversation about the entire range of possibilities and the consequences of our choices, gradually leading to autonomy. This does not mean we allow our child to make all the decisions; it simply means that we are engaging them in the decision-making process. We do this for two reasons: (1) because they will be more willing to engage in activities they have chosen, and (2) because we want them to learn how to make good choices. Just as when they are little, it is up to us to feed them healthy food, but as they get older, we need to help them learn to make healthy eating choices for themselves.

If we want our children to learn how to make good choices, why wouldn't we engage them in the decision-making process from the very beginning? In fact, we do. We engage them by sharing with them the reasons for our decisions. We say things like, "If you want to learn piano, you need to practice every day just like we practice reading. How about we play for five minutes every day after you come home and have a snack? That way you'll have plenty of time to hang out with your friends." As a teacher of a young guitar student who resists using their left-hand pinky (as they all do), I would say, "We need to build up strength in your fourth finger, so I have a really cool exercise to take your pinky to the gym!" I would not say, "Do you want to work on getting a stronger pinky?" nor would I say, "Do these exercises because I assigned them."

It isn't reasonable or fair to ask children to make decisions about situations and behaviors about which they have no information. If I showed my five-year-old daughter two book covers and asked her, "Which book would you rather read before bed, *The Cat in the Hat* or *Moby Dick*?" she might very well pick the story about the whale! Similarly, a young beginner may believe they are ready to play a very difficult piece or perform in a high-pressure environment. On the other hand, they may be terrified to try a harder piece or play for a few friends. The bottom line is that they have very little information about the true difficulty of the music or the relative pressure of the recital. Once they have experienced these things, then we can enter into an intelligent conversation.

Every time a new family comes to our school to sign up, there will come a moment in the registration process where I discuss with the parent the need for regular practice. Most of the time, upon hearing this, the parent will turn to his child and say, "Did you hear that, Alice? Can you commit to practicing every day?" The thing is, whether she says yes or no, she has no idea what she's agreeing to or refusing to do. I understand that the parent simply wants to get the child's verbal agreement before signing on, but in my experience, children rarely remember such conversations for more than a few minutes, let alone a few years.

Practice Tips for Developing Discipline

This is not a book focused solely on tips and tricks for practice. Plenty of those exist, and they are great. Nevertheless, a big part of developing your own personalized style of discipline is trying out what has worked for others and seeing if you can modify it in some way to fit your own style. It isn't unlike developing your own style of clothing. Most kids will go through a period of trying out different "looks" until they find something they like. And just like their style of dress, their style of discipline will evolve with them as they mature.

Nearly every tip in Stage One can be converted into a conversation to create a tip for Stage Two. For example, instead of removing roadblocks for our children, we can observe how certain roadblocks make it difficult to practice and discuss alternatives with them. When

my daughter was in third grade, practice was becoming increasingly difficult because whenever she would practice, she could hear her friends playing outside the window. We discussed practicing in the mornings, and ultimately it was largely her decision to switch to a half-day school that holds classes only in the afternoons so that she could practice in the mornings and have her afternoons and evenings free to play with her friends.

The tips and tricks here are specific to young children who

Photo courtesy of Aarti Kaul

have been playing for a couple years and are ready to take their playing, and therefore their practicing, to the next level. These suggestions go beyond transforming Stage One tips into conversations (as important as that is) to beginning to build the foundations for a highly disciplined individual who knows how to push his own unique motivational buttons.

> Discipline is all the little things we do every day that give us the capacity to do the hard work that creates change.

Tip #1: Discussions Around Ownership

Stage Two is all about our gradually relinquishing ownership of all the important aspects of disciplined behavior to our kids. As we discussed at the beginning of this chapter, this mostly involves transforming our own decisions as parents and teachers into conversations with our children about everything from goals to schedules to how we set up the practice area. An equal part of gradually giving our children ownership, however, is expressing recognition of their accomplishments. If the outcome of a conversation about goals was that a child chose to play in the school talent show, then when he completes that goal, his parent can not only express her pride in how well he played, but also ask how all his hard work prepared him for that day. Not just, "Wow! You were amazing! I wish I had your talent," but rather, "Wow! That was amazing! I feel like you've been practicing differently these past few months; did that have an effect on how you played today?"

> **MUSIC LESSON TO LIFE LESSON**
> Don't celebrate the end result without acknowledging all the blood, sweat, and tears it took to get there. Reminding your child of the process will make the praise feel more genuine and will encourage that process to become a pattern.

Tip #2: Have Honest Conversations About What Is Most Motivating

Staying highly motivated toward a single goal over a long period of time is extremely rare for most individuals. Most people mistakenly believe that the secret to focusing intently on improving in a particular field is simply finding our special area of interest. They believe each person is born with a predilection to love one subject intensively, and our goal in life should be to find that one area and "follow our bliss." While I won't deny that — in retrospect, it sometimes feels as though music was my "one true passion" — I think it is more honest to say that there were many areas that piqued my interest as a child, and music happened to provide me with the right set of challenges and rewarding experiences to eventually garner my devotion. Once I had devoted myself to music, I was fortunate enough to encounter one motivating opportunity after another: playing with adults around a campfire, forming a band with friends, going to music camp, applying to college, entering competitions, returning to my home town to play a sold-out concert …

Try to make a habit of asking your child what she finds most exciting about what she is doing and encourage her to share this information with her teacher. For some kids, it is the creativity of composing and improvising; for others it is performing; for still others it is learning new songs. For many, it is a little of everything. The trick is to keep asking the question, and eventually she will start asking herself the question.

MUSIC LESSON TO LIFE LESSON
Help your child to identify what makes him tick and use that information to find the fuel for intense engagement.

Tip #3: Teach Them Time Management

One of the things I frequently tell parents is that if they solve issues around practice they will solve many other problems inherent in family life. How many otherwise pleasant mornings have become stressful and frustrating because of the number of times we had to remind our kids to brush their teeth, double-check their homework, pack their backpacks, remember to take their lunch, and, oh, let's squeeze in a last practice of that sonatina because your lesson is this afternoon?

Teaching our children the skills of time management, prioritization, and making meaningful progress toward goals isn't just essential for music practice — it is essential for life. But, as the great piano pedagogue Frances Clark was fond of saying, "Teaching is not telling." That is, telling our kids they need to make a schedule, telling them they need to prioritize, and telling them they will never achieve anything meaningful if they don't set a meaningful goal is not the same thing as teaching them. Teaching involves little steps, small trials, observation of the results, praise, and corrections along the way.

We can start by making a general outline of our daily routine together. After a few adjustments and praise for when this is working well, maybe we can experiment with ways of getting music theory and schoolwork done during commutes to and from school or extracurricular activities. Most kids will be resistant to the idea of using their previously unstructured time to do focused work. Accustomed to using time in the car or waiting rooms to play on their phones or daydream, they may feel like this time is their only chance to be free of adults telling them what to do. If we connect getting homework done to getting more quality time playing with friends and achieving goals they have set for themselves, however, they can often become feverishly devoted to knocking out "busy-work" whenever they get the chance.

This is not a book on time management; the main point is that a child who is motivated to experiment with different approaches to finishing the work she needs to accomplish in the time she has will be much more successful, have more free time, and will likely need less nagging than a child who actively avoids responsibility (as most do). In Stage One, we set up the structures that lead to success; in Stage Two, we teach them to find their own structures.

WEEKLY SCHEDULE							
	SUN	MON	TUE	WED	THU	FRI	SAT
7:30 AM		chores	chores	chores	chores	chores	
8:00 AM-3:00 PM		school	school	school	school	school	soccer
3:00 PM - 3:30 PM		snack	snack	snack	snack	snack	
3:30 PM - 4:00 PM		practice	practice	piano lesson	practice		practice
4:00 PM - 4:30 PM		←——————— homework ———————→					
4:30 PM - 5:30 PM			soccer		soccer		
5:30 PM - 7:00 PM							

Tip #4: Teach Them to Communicate Their Needs

When kids are very young, they have trouble identifying specific causes of their discomfort, and they certainly lack communication skills. We don't expect a toddler to come up to us and say, "I need my diaper changed; then I'd like to go down for a nap, and afterward, maybe we can play some together." So we, as good attentive parents, learn to

MUSIC LESSON TO LIFE LESSON
I cannot begin to tell you how many times students who overcame their struggles with music practice by implementing a schedule also experienced simultaneous improvement in their grades at school. Parents often find that the need to create some order in their day created space for other things as well, like homework and even play!

recognize their needs and frequently step in to express those needs to others for our children. This, of course, is entirely appropriate while they are very young. As they grow, however, we need to help them learn to express their needs to their friends and teachers in appropriate ways.

A good teacher will make a habit of asking his students how they are doing and what might help them learn better. An exceptional teacher may be able to sense most of his students' needs intuitively and make adjustments on the fly. Nevertheless, no parent or teacher is a perfect mind-reader, able to know what students are thinking, feeling, or what their needs are. Furthermore, even if he could perfectly guess his students' needs all the time, he would, in fact, be depriving his students of the opportunity to develop an essential communication skill.

This is particularly difficult, and particularly important, for very shy children. My own daughter seems to think it is an intolerable disruption to ask her classroom teacher if she can go to the bathroom or sharpen her pencil, let alone express that she's bored with the material and would like to learn something more challenging and more interesting. I don't claim to be an expert at getting shy kids to express themselves, but our approach has been to try to help our daughter feel comfortable, go with her to teacher meetings, and ask her to prepare ahead of time several things to say.

When it comes to staying motivated and making steady improvement, we need to accept the fact that we will encounter significant obstacles, some of which will likely seem insurmountable. Nobody ever achieved anything of value without a struggle. Unless they have the ability to express their needs clearly, collaborate on a plan to try a variety of solutions, and stay committed to that plan, our children are likely to take the easiest solution whenever they are struggling: quit.

> *MUSIC LESSON TO LIFE LESSON*
> Children who can talk to their music teachers about what
> is difficult or de-motivating can talk to their other teachers
> and friends about their needs and desires.

Tip #5: Getting Started Really Is Half the Battle

Practicing is a lot like taking a bath for most kids. It is a battle
to get them in, but then you can't get them out! Recently, prior to
practicing piano, my daughter came into my room, leaned against the
wall dejectedly, and said, "I just don't feel like practicing! Can I just
do a little and then we can play a game together?" I said, "Sure, but
I know your piano teacher wants to hear the end of 'Cat and Mouse'
learned well this week." I told her to do just 15 minutes, and then we
could do something together.

> The main difference between those who are highly
> successful and those who are not is this: The successful
> ones keep starting — even when they don't feel like it.

Thirty minutes later, she was still digging into the tricky runs and
chords that make up this devilishly fun piece of music. The truth is,
she loves this piece, but we had just gotten back from a vacation that
included zip lining and playing with our new puppy in a creek. So,
she hadn't played piano for several days, was probably rusty, didn't
remember her pieces, and most importantly compared to that vacation,
any practice was going to seem like a chore! But, once she got started
and her fingers began to fly over the keys, the memory of how good it
feels to play well started coming back to her.

After she practiced, she came back and said, "Was that completely
terrible?"

I said, "That was awesome! Not only could I hear the cat chasing
the mouse, but I heard you breaking it down into little pieces and
working each separately. Nice work."

Then I went on to remind her how common it is to not want to
play after a break of a couple days. It is just hard to get started again,

but once we do, we realize how fun it was. This is the main difference between those who are highly successful and those who are not: The successful ones keep starting — even when they don't feel like it.

MUSIC LESSON TO LIFE LESSON
Inspiration leads to a desire to practice. And practice leads to inspiration.

Tip #6: Teach Them About Sleep

Anders Ericsson's observations of the violinists at the Berlin Academy of Music made the "10,000-hour rule" famous (the top violinists had mostly practiced around 10,000 hours by the time they got to that stage in their career — over 5,000 hours more, on average, than the "very good" violinists). But that was just one of his observations. Another one that has gotten very little press was the stunning statistic that the top violinists got an average of five hours more sleep per week than their nearest competitors — mostly in the form of naps.

The instinct of many "driven" students is always to work harder and put in longer hours, often cutting into sleep time. In fact, recent studies have shown that under 15 percent of high school students are getting enough sleep, and, as is now well known, lack of sleep significantly reduces "your ability to learn, listen, concentrate, and solve problems" — all things at the top of the list for productive practice (National Sleep Foundation).

My own daughter hates naps. She stopped napping around age two and never looked back. Like many "intense" children I have taught, she tries to squeeze as much out of every day as possible. I have made some inroads with her by sharing Ericsson's research on the top violinists, but I still can't get her to take naps the way I love to. With younger children, it is essential that we prioritize sleep. As kids get older, we need to teach them that cutting into sleep to practice or study is an ineffective strategy since they are reducing rather than increasing their ability to think clearly.

Another benefit of sleep is the effect it can have on memory.

Studies have shown that if you practice a musical passage intensely one day, you may not be able to remember it right away. After a good night's sleep, however, you are much more likely to be able to recall the passage accurately. Next time your child is struggling with her practice, encourage her to sleep on it and try it again the next day. She may find it much easier!

Tip #7: Teach Them about Slumps and Slump Recovery

Slumps happen to everyone in every field. We need to come prepared with an anti-slump arsenal so that we can get over it quickly and get back to loving what we are doing.

Most of my students eventually need guidance on how to recover from a slump. They may have been going along quite well for several months or even years, but eventually a series of events (or maybe nothing at all) conspires to sap their interest and energy. Perhaps a student goes skiing over winter break, sprains a wrist, and then, just as he is healing, he catches the flu and has to miss another week (true story). By now it is almost February, and I haven't seen him for six weeks. When he comes back, he informs me that maybe guitar just isn't for him. He's lost interest and wants to try something new.

> Everyone who is great at anything has had to go through ups and downs. The difference is they didn't stop when they hit a slump.

In cases like this, I usually empathize with the student and ask him to try an experiment with me. I suggest that he views this as a slump recovery research project. I tell him that no matter what you want to be great at, there will always come a time when you lose interest and want to quit. If he still wants to quit after he has tried several of the slump recovery techniques that have worked in the past for other students, as well as a few of his own, I will completely support the decision.

Here are a few of the slump recovery tricks that my students and I have come up with:

- Make a playlist and listen to music constantly every day.
- Make a list of all the things you used to love about your instrument.
- Set an exciting goal.
- Put a photo that reminds you of that goal where you will see it every day.
- Spend more time around others who are excited about playing.
- Find a new time or new way to practice (for example, three short practices instead of one long one).
- Buy a new instrument or other exciting piece of musical equipment.

The point is, everyone who is great at anything has had to go through ups and downs. The difference is they didn't stop when they hit a slump.

Tip #8: Encourage Them to Sign Up for Something Big

While there are probably some parents who hold their children back from trying to accomplish big, scary goals, the more common situation is simply that the child pulls back and the parent, both wanting to "respect the child's wishes" and, frankly, too busy to contemplate taking on another obligation, agrees that this particular goal is probably too much. If you trust your teacher, and she has recommended that your child shoot for a higher goal, then I say, "Go ahead and push!"

In my experience, many, if not most, kids will innately resist trying something new (e.g., a new food, a new teacher, or a new goal). This is normal and probably served us well evolutionarily when it came to surviving in the wild. In the relatively safe context of learning a musical instrument, however, this strategy will likely backfire. When I first recommend that a child perform in public, he often thinks he is not ready — even though he has no idea what it will be like! It's like the new-food rule: You have to eat two full bites before you can tell me if you like it or not.

Big goals are like throwing fuel on the fire — not only for children, but for professional musicians as well. The teachers I work with often have a good laugh that our students make more progress in the two weeks leading up to recital time than the rest of the whole year combined! There is nothing like a nice, clear performance goal to clarify what we need to do in the practice room to really perfect our pieces, solve our technical issues, and overcome whatever roadblocks are standing in our way. For myself, I know that I will practice twice as much and with twice as much focus once I have set the date for a concert. That is one of the main reasons I still perform: to make myself practice.

MUSIC LESSON TO LIFE LESSON
Committing yourself to clear, attainable goals just outside your comfort zone focuses your mind and maximizes results.

Tip #9: Allow Them to Fail

I once had a student whose mother would not let her perform even though she was perfectly ready. Her explanation was that if her daughter performed badly, it could damage her love of music forever. As a fellow tennis enthusiast, she used an analogy she thought I'd understand: "If she plays badly, it will be like losing to a player you know you should be able to beat. It can set you back forever!" I agreed that overcoming a difficult performance can be like losing a tennis match you feel you should have won, but in another way: The best players are those who deal effectively with defeat and learn from it.

Many parents (and teachers!) want to protect their children from failure, both large and small — whether it is forgetting the lyrics in the middle of a big performance or stumbling through a scale passage at home because you haven't mastered the fingering. Sooner or later, all students will struggle. Parents and teachers who treat this as a learning experience that is normal and expected give the child the respect of being a capable human being who can handle disappointment. When we hold our children back from attempting difficult challenges, we subtly give them the message that they can't handle difficult emotions. If we give them this message often enough, they will begin to believe it.

When my daughter performed her first concert on both guitar and piano (not simultaneously), she struggled with one of the piano pieces, completely forgetting the ending and being unable to find the last note. Afterward, she had to face audience members who mostly fawned over her and told her how talented she was. When my wife and I got a chance to be alone with her, we didn't lie to her and tell her she had played great. We honestly told her that we and the audience both were moved by her expressive playing, and that anyone who plays enough concerts will eventually have a mental slip. It has happened to literally every professional musician. "The audience isn't coming to the concert to hear you play all the notes right," we told her. "They are coming to hear you tell a story with music. And you did that." She was still sad for a little while (as anyone who takes pride in her work would be), but she seemed to let go of perfection a little that day, and because she wasn't thinking about the possibility that she might blank out during a performance, I think that helped her concentrate on her music and have fewer memory slips in concerts since then.

Tip #10: Allow Them to Own Their Success

Some parents and teachers feel that any unconditional praise will lead to laziness. If a child performs beautifully, they feel the need to point out that he did not smile when he bowed. If the judges in a competition award him second prize, they tell the child he could have gotten first if only he had practiced more.

While striving for excellence is valuable, one of the best things about the arts is that it is subjective. This means that you can never truly know whose performance is best. Some people view this as a drawback, but I believe it is a strength when building our children into adults most likely to succeed and be happy in life.

The greatest success will be had by those who stick with an endeavor, keep their minds open and curious, and utilize all the tools at their disposal to learn more effectively (the three pillars). Learners who are obsessed with being the best are more likely to shy away from experiences in which they are unlikely to shine. Unfortunately for them, these are the very experiences that are most likely to allow them to grow. When our children make a breakthrough in the practice room or on stage, it is worth noting and even celebrating. There will be plenty of time to work on improving later.

I am not suggesting that we embrace the "participant award" mentality that everyone is a winner, no matter how badly she played, and I don't believe that all musical performances are of equal value. A child who rarely practiced and then tortures the audience with a screechy, out-of-tune violin performance of "Twinkle, Twinkle, Little Star" at the school talent show should not be praised for what a great job she did. But anyone who put in the hours of focused practice to do her best deserves to have her moment of complete admiration and respect.

7

STAGE THREE:
SELF-MOTIVATION

"You may give them your love but not your thoughts,
For they have their own thoughts."
– KAHLIL GIBRAN

Once a love of making music and good habits of disciplined behavior are solidly in place, most students will begin to find their own way in the world of music. Especially if they have had the opportunity to explore many forms of music and connect their music-making to their external world. Nearly every student I have ever taught that stuck around and practiced for five or more years (and frequently much less!) found something that sparked his interest. For some, it became a relaxing hobby, for others an all-consuming passion, but for each the discovery was both unique and often surprising.

This final phase of development can simultaneously be the most rewarding and the most difficult for parents. It is thrilling to see your child find her unique voice and begin investing time and energy into creating something truly personal. At the same time, the patterns of behavior that were so helpful in the earlier years are often rejected by children seeking to do things on their own. If you experienced success sitting next to your child on the piano bench in the early years, it can be difficult when those same sessions turn into fights, tears, and power struggles. It is time to allow them to practice their own way, in their own time, and set their own goals.

At this stage, there isn't much we parents can do except support and celebrate. Not that that is any small task: Support can be expensive and time consuming, especially if your child becomes serious about music. Lessons, high-quality instruments, transportation to rehearsals and events, competitions, auditions, and more can easily add up to a small fortune. Of course, at this stage it is not only possible but helpful to engage him in considering how to afford paying for his own goals. When my daughter was ready for a truly concert-quality guitar, we asked around, visited luthiers together, and found the best instruments were in the $8,000–$12,000 range. In order to help us pay for it and help her learn to take responsibility, my wife and I asked her to perform a concert on both piano and guitar and ask for donations toward the new instrument. She raised about $500, which was a small fraction of the overall cost, but it was a meaningful challenge for her and was helpful to us.

Musicians' Stage-Three Stories

Max's Story

Quite some time ago, after several years of studying classical, blues, and folk styles (partially with me and partially with another teacher), Max saw a Bluegrass band playing on TV. He was transfixed. From that moment forward, he studied all music as a way to build his skills and understanding of the guitar so that he could become the best Bluegrass guitarist he could be. His practice took on a new focus and purpose, and he became unstoppable. I am proud to say that Max now plays professionally as the lead guitarist of the Hot Pickin' 57.

Sofia's Story

Sofia had studied classical guitar for five years before she switched to my studio. She had been quite serious at one point, even taking third prize in an international guitar competition at the age of eight, but by the time she started with me, she was struggling to find either the time or the motivation to practice. Her mom, who usually brought her to the lessons, was clearly frustrated with Sofia's lack of commitment. During the lessons, she mostly wanted to play music she had learned years before and recoiled from learning new pieces, getting feedback, or reading music. From my perspective, most of the energy and time available for Sofia's practice was being used up in battling against those whom she perceived as trying to control her.

I decided to take a radical approach with her: I refused to assign her any new pieces of music to practice and refused to critique her playing during the lesson. What I told her was that I was there to help with anything she wanted, but she was in charge. This took quite a leap of faith from her parents, who continued paying for lessons that could have ended up being nothing but sitting in silence! Gradually, though, Sofia started bringing me interesting projects, including new classical pieces and some remarkably creative songs she had written. I would listen and ask, "Is there anything you would like my help on?" and off we would go. Her lessons became some of the most artistic and inspiring moments of my week, and I always looked forward to seeing what she would bring.

Today she continues to compose, has formed a band, and manages to find time to get out to open-mike opportunities between studying for her college classes. Here is how she described her musical life to me: "Music has always been important to me, but lately it has become one of the biggest parts of who I am and what I do with my time, and you played a big part in fostering my love for it. As I got older, particularly through the pressure I felt in band, music became a huge source of stress for me, but you helped guitar remain something that I genuinely enjoyed, and I am so grateful for that."

Stephen's Story

Stephen is a multi-talented guitarist and teacher who came to work at my academy in 2016 and who happens to exemplify the three stages: He started young just playing for fun, grew up in a community of exceptional guitarists and musicians, and went on to find his own voice playing and teaching in a wide variety of contexts.

My biggest jump was when I was 15. I had started working on Villa Lobos' *Chôros No. 1*, which I had been listening to on my car rides to guitar lessons for years. I was dying to play it for a long time and was thrilled when [my teacher] Alan [Johnston] said I could learn it. I learned it very quickly, and it brought me to one of my highest levels of playing.

Another reason I practiced this piece so hard was the Schubert Club Scholarship Competition. Many of Alan's students had won it in the past, and I had competed a couple times and gotten second place or no prize. I was determined to win it that year and practiced hard with more focus than ever. I did end up winning the competition and as a result got to play on Minnesota Public Radio.

I think the jump in my playing was a result of loving the piece I was studying and having the goal of winning this competition. It was a mix of love for the art with the pressure of the competition. I practiced with joy and with purpose, and my playing improved markedly because of it. — Stephen Krishnan

The Three Pillars in the Later Years

Learner's Mindset

If our children reach a point of self-motivation through the application of personalized discipline, they are highly likely to already be engaged with a learner's mindset. After all, they probably would not be self-motivated if they weren't also curious and engaged. Nevertheless, there are two pitfalls I have observed over the years that can drain or even completely derail a budding musician at this stage.

PROJECTING OUR OWN HOPES AND DREAMS ONTO OUR CHILDREN

As innocent and natural as this may seem, pushing our children to follow our dreams only stunts their opportunity to express their own vision for themselves. Even when we outwardly say, "All I want is for you to be happy," if we are secretly hoping they will learn to play the traditional music of our culture or get a scholarship to Harvard, it will subtly influence our interactions in a negative way. The curiosity of a learner's mindset is undermined when our children are subconsciously thinking about our hopes and dreams for them. The energy and commitment needed to stick with difficult problems is sapped away when they are drawing on our dreams rather than their own for motivation.

One professional pianist in the Bloom study noted, "I had a very special background that I think is important: namely, parents who had no motives other than fantastic interest in their son and what he could do, and enjoying that. It wasn't that 'Well, he's going to have to learn to grow up and be a concert pianist' " (75). In fact, this unattached support turns out to be more the norm than the pianist in the study seems to believe. Many of the greatest musicians in history were allowed to grow with support, but without expectations.

COOKIE-CUTTER TEACHERS

Many teachers (even excellent ones) have a standard set of exercises, pieces, performances, and festivals they want all their students to do. This may be fine for Stages One and Two, and even Stage Three if the child happens to be a natural fit for this approach. But for most maturing musicians, this will begin to feel more like a straitjacket than a supportive learning environment and will have the same effect as parental aspirations. A great teacher will know how to adjust to being more of a coach than an instructor: offering guidance and assistance in accomplishing goals articulated by the young musician.

Grit

Young musicians in this stage of development possess a combination of exceptional skill, good habits, strong willpower, and, most of all, a passion for what they do, making them some of the "grittiest" individuals in our society. I believe that this, more than anything else, explains why there is such a strong correlation between music study and good grades (among other things). The only danger here is one of *too* much grit.

Some young people at this stage are so driven to excel at everything they set their minds to, so unwilling to give up on any project, that they completely overload themselves. My own daughter is currently struggling with whether she should continue to participate in her choir even though it no longer brings her much joy or sparks her interest. "I don't quit," she says when we suggest that maybe she would be happier if she had more time to spend with her friends. Other high-performing students maintain straight A's at the top high schools and enter language, dance, tennis, business, and engineering competitions while striving to keep up their interest in music. I have witnessed breakdowns, eating disorders, sleep disorders, anxiety, and more, all due to an unwillingness to "give up" on anything. Being stressed out, missing sleep, and worrying all the time does not lead to higher levels of success. Focused, intelligent, energetic action is what leads to success.

Interestingly, very few of the top performers in any given field were truly excellent at more than a couple things. My advice to my own students is this: Pursue one passion, balance it out with a hobby, maintain good grades, and *enjoy yourself as much as possible.* Joy is the source of our strength, our energy, and our wisdom. This is not some woo-woo advice to "follow your bliss"; this is practical advice about how to live a successful life. From time to time, this means having a difficult conversation with a student I love who I think should either give up music (at least for a while) or cut back on something else in his life. If he chooses to give up music, I will be just as happy and love him just the same, knowing he will apply the lessons of personalized discipline that we have practiced all these years to whatever endeavor he pursues.

> Stress doesn't lead to success. Focused, intelligent, energetic action leads to success.

Deliberate Practice

This is the stage when many students truly begin to understand the power of deliberate-practice techniques. When they were young, they had to be led by teachers and parents to practice effectively, through games, charts, rewards, and the like. As they grew older, they may have followed the practice suggestions of their teachers as part of their evolving discipline, but only when they reach the stage of self-motivation do they actually get the full benefit of deliberate practice.

The reason students can't achieve maximum results from deliberate-practice techniques when they are younger is that they are mostly "following instructions." They generally have a lack of what is known as "metacognition" (the ability to understand the larger process of learning): the "why" behind the choices of "how" to practice. When students begin to choose which practice techniques to use because *they themselves* perceive a weakness in their playing, their practice becomes infinitely more effective. Don't get me wrong: Following the instructions of an exceptional teacher can get you quite far. You can learn to play many songs and techniques very well. But when you fully own the process, can solve problems on your own, and create a vision of the music that comes directly from you rather than your teacher — that is when things really start to take off.

Many students don't truly grasp this until well into a music degree, if then. They have been led, step by step, to competence, but never had the chance to explore for themselves how to become truly excellent musicians. For myself, when I finally decided to practice with intention, I began by doing every practice technique that I had ever heard was used by a great guitarist. Unfortunately, that didn't take into account my own personality, goals, or circumstances. First you must understand the problem you are trying to solve, then you choose the most effective tool for fixing the problem, then (most likely) you fail, try something else, and repeat until you make progress. It is a process of exploration and discovery followed by intelligent repetition, not a mindless execution of someone else's personal approach.

CAN OLDER BEGINNERS BENEFIT FROM DELIBERATE PRACTICE?

Given the facts that (1) older children are often resistant to playing the types of games suggested above in Stage One: Loving Practice and Establishing Habits, and (2) we know that deliberate practice is so difficult as to be demoralizing to all but the most highly motivated students, is there any value in trying to get adolescent and preadolescent beginners to engage in deliberate practice? Is it worth our time and effort to engage in the most challenging practice techniques when it might turn them off from music forever?

The answer, I believe, is a "Yes" — with a caveat. "Yes," because who doesn't want to make the most rapid improvement possible? I often tell my students, "We

> *"Somewhere along the line, the child must become possessed by music, by the sudden desire to play, to excel.... Suddenly the child begins to work, and in retrospect the first five or six years seem like Kinderspiel, fooling around."*
>
> **— Isaac Stern**

can fix this problem in five minutes of careful, thoughtful practice, or we can spend the rest of the lesson playing it over and over, and it might get better. Which do you choose?" Not surprisingly, nobody has ever chosen to play it over and over.

The problem is that the more effective the practice technique, the more difficult and exhausting it is likely to be. If someone showed me, an amateur tennis player, the workout Roger Federer used throughout his career to reach the peak physical and technical excellence that made him the greatest player on earth, I would do it happily. I suspect, however, that after a couple of days, or maybe just a couple of hours, I would want to quit tennis. I enjoy tennis, but I simply don't have the level of passion, commitment, and belief that I can be one of the best tennis players in the world to engage in that kind of rigorous practice day after day. This isn't to say that I wouldn't benefit from a 15-minute drill lifted out of Federer's practice routine.

In any field, we can all learn more effective practice techniques from the experts in order to focus our learning. We just need to monitor how our energy levels are doing after each practice. For myself, at this stage in my career, I am happy if I can play the music I love beautifully and expressively. I am not looking to extend my technical prowess, the speed of my scales, or my ability to memorize long pieces of music the way I was 20 years ago when I was in college. So, in my practice sessions these days, I will frequently play through several pieces I know well, and then turn to a new piece, carefully fingering, analyzing, slow-practicing, and problem-solving a short section, and then call it a day. All in all, I may have spent ten minutes of an hour-long practice doing the hard work of deliberate practice. It is a little like circuit training at the gym: One day you focus on one set of muscles intensely, but also do some cardio stretching. Not everything should be hard work every day.

Furthermore, it is my belief from spending years around some of the finest artists, talking to them, and surreptitiously listening in on their practice, that even the best in the world use the techniques of deliberate practice less than 50 percent of the time. Some of my best teachers have admonished me to "choose to get better every time you sit down to practice." But some of these same world-class players will share that they enjoy watching sports while playing through their pieces (just as I do!).

The caveat, then, is this: Encourage deliberate practice while also encouraging balance, breaks, and fun. The art of balancing growth and continued love of music lies in the ability to balance challenge with joyful music-making. The better an older beginner knows himself and his goals, the better he can choose the right music and technical exercises to make maximum improvement today while keeping his motivation high.

MUSIC LESSON TO LIFE LESSON
Life is all about balance. Taking mental breaks by alternating between moments of intense focus and moments of pure fun keep us from getting burned out.

TIME TO STEP BACK

Whether they are beginning, intermediate, or advanced music students, the greatest hindrance to older kids' developing their own approach to deliberate practice and enjoying the ensuing benefits, ironically, is parents and teachers who over-prescribe how to practice. Not teaching students how to practice effectively is a problem, but never letting them discover what works best for them is a crippling disaster.

This is probably the biggest challenge in our family right now. I truly wish that I could magically forget everything I know about practice so that I wouldn't be tempted to suggest to my daughter which deliberate practice techniques she should use. She has progressed through the stage of loving practice, has developed solid habits, and now she needs the space to make her own choices about how and what to practice. My best choices in this realm are usually to go listen to music in another room and simply be supportive the rest of the time. For this reason, I recommend that parents not read Appendix B (Deliberate Practice for the Advanced Student). If your child progresses to the level where she is beginning to take ownership of her development and is eager to take her playing to the next level, perhaps she will be interested in reading about what other great musicians have done to achieve amazing levels of ability and artistry. Perhaps not.

Either way, it is her journey now.

8

EPILOGUE

When I began writing this book I saw it as a list of useful tips for parents. After all, that is what I had been asked for and had been dispensing for years. Why not collect them all in one place?

But somewhere along the way, it turned into something much more. Yes, I discovered how to make practice more fun and effective for my daughter (and myself!). Yes, I came to understand why getting better is so intensely difficult, and yes, I came to understand how the right mindset can make all the difference. But what is truly amazing to me is that it has not only been a journey of understanding how we can all grow our abilities and enjoy the process, but it has also been a process of coming to love myself, my students, and my daughter for who each of us is and simultaneously for who we are becoming.

When I was in my late teens and twenties, I knew I wanted to be a professional musician, and that drove me to practice and study at a furious (and sometimes even physically harmful) rate. I had to make significant and definite progress toward being a great guitarist every day, or I didn't like myself. If I took time to do something fun with friends, after several hours, I would begin to feel that I was being lazy and not achieving my goals. If I had fun "messing around" on guitar for a while without making serious improvement, I would chastise myself. Even if I practiced in a focused and diligent way, but then my performance didn't live up to expectations, I would feel all my efforts had been worthless. I had tied all my self-worth into the quality of my playing, and that made it extremely difficult to be happy for any length of time.

Later, when my wife and I opened our music school together, I had much the same feeling: Either we were hitting it out of the park, or we were complete failures. When something would go wrong, it didn't feel like an opportunity to learn; it felt like I was letting myself and my employees down. In times like that, it was difficult to motivate myself to get back to work, to look for creative solutions, and to move forward joyfully. It wasn't until I truly embraced the idea that this is a lifelong journey — that I will continue to make mistakes, learn new things, and find new ways to engage (even when I don't feel like it) — that our business really started to take off.

As a parent, I know I subconsciously passed this quality-performance bias on to my daughter during the early years of her study. Even though I took all the steps I knew to make practice fun, eliminate roadblocks, and supercharge her motivation, underneath it all I sensed that her primary motivation was to reach my own unreachable standards (the same standards that had been unreachable for me!). As I have learned to allow her to follow her own path and step back from judging her progress, not only has she begun to enjoy practice more, but I have also been able to enjoy hearing her practice.

Finally, as a teacher, I now appreciate that every student and every family are on a journey to discover how to make joyful, disciplined practice a part of their lives. I don't expect parents to show up on the first day knowing how to support the music lessons, and I don't pretend to know exactly what will work best for them. I simply want to share this journey with them and keep an open mind so that all of us can "stick with it and together find a way to make it fun."

Not long ago, hearing the sounds of my daughter's imperfect guitar practice, my heart filled with joy. The notes bore the unmistakable phrasing of someone who loves music. Not perfect, but something better. Something human. The striving to be better than we are and the love of who we are now blend together in a higher level of love than I had ever known was possible.

APPENDIX A

CHOOSING THE RIGHT TEACHER

Choosing the right teacher for your child is a daunting task. Most parents are not trained musicians and, even if they are, will have trouble judging quickly if a teacher is going to be right for their family. In my experience, most parents err too far to one side or the other in picking a teacher. Either they are so picky that they are never happy with any teacher and do harm to their child by constantly switching from one teacher to another as soon as they perceive the slightest flaw, or they are accepting of whatever teacher comes along because they heard good things from a friend or because the teacher lives nearby.

Effective teaching is hard. My wife and I founded our music school with the express purpose of continuing our lifelong pursuit of improving ourselves as teachers because, even after completing advanced degrees in music performance and education, in which we were supervised by expert teachers for several years each, we believed we were just scratching the surface. Fifteen years later, I still feel that way. Parents are often surprised that someone with an advanced degree and 25 years of experience would need to seek out additional training, critique his own teaching on video, read books on teaching, and spend an average of an hour every day planning for lessons. We do this because teaching well is extremely difficult. We enjoy doing this because we have created an environment and a set of motivations for ourselves that make the discipline of improving our teaching a source of joy (sound familiar?).

9 Things Great Teachers Do

In the study of great teaching, one thing has become abundantly clear: There is no such thing as a perfect teacher. This is not only because effective teaching requires excellence in a vast array of skills and knowledge, but also because a great teacher for one student may be a terrible teacher for another, and vice versa. Below is a list of things that great teachers do (and at which they excel). I have never met someone who was good at them *all*, so we have to pick several that we absolutely require ("Respect the student" comes to mind) and others that we may have to supplement or augment on our own.

1. *Respect the Student*

Good teachers respect their students, getting to know each as an individual and putting the child's development into a joyful, skilled musician and happy human being above all else.

2. *Possess Extensive Expertise*

Effective music instruction requires having a clear understanding of every aspect of musical excellence, from technique, to style, to musicianship, to theory. Teachers must be able to articulate this understanding in ways appropriate to the age and ability of each of their students. A good teacher need not be the best musician in the world, but he needs to be skilled enough to discern what constitutes excellence in his students.

3. *Assess Students Accurately*

It's important for music teachers to be skilled at assessing their students' technical, musical, emotional, and motivational needs. In order to make progress, the teacher must "begin where the student is." If the teacher misjudges the student's ability, she will be unable to design an appropriate course of study.

4. *Work from an Effective Sequence of Materials Appropriate to the Student*

There are many books available for learning each instrument, and none of them are perfect for any child. All of them (including those I have written myself) must, at the very least, be supplemented to meet the needs of the child. Many methods, unfortunately, are seriously flawed in some way: Either the progression of skills is too fast or too slow, the material is uninteresting, the technique is damaging to physical development, or some other serious problem. A good teacher must overcome the flaws of the method book.

5. Give Effective Feedback to the Student

This means providing feedback that is appropriate, well-timed, delivered in a manner to which the student is receptive, and, above all, results in improvement in the student's playing. This is exceptionally difficult because one is never quite sure what words or tasks will magically create a breakthrough for the student. A great deal of experience and good intuition are the best guides, but even then, it is easy to fall short.

6. Teach the Child to Learn on Her Own

A good teacher will assist the child in transferring the skills she has learned to new contexts so that she may begin to learn on her own. All great teachers wish to "teach themselves out of a job." If the teacher approaches each lesson by showing the student where to put her fingers to play this or that song, it is unlikely that the student will eventually be able to figure out new songs on her own. If, on the other hand, the teacher provides the student with the tools for learning, helps her to feel empowered to learn new things on her own, and gives her opportunities to practice learning on her own, then the student may one day surpass the teacher.

Of course, an even higher level of transference is to help the child to understand how she achieved excellence in music and transfer those learning skills to other areas of her life.

7. Provide Motivating and Appropriate Performance Experiences

Without the motivation that comes from playing in groups, recognition at talent shows, performing on recitals, and other opportunities to shine, even the most dedicated student is likely to lose interest.

8. *Build Well-Rounded Skills*

The famed composer and music educator Zoltán Kodály said, "The characteristics of a good musician are a well-trained ear, a well-trained mind, a well-trained heart, and a well-trained hand. All four parts must develop together in constant equilibrium" (197). This doesn't refer to a teacher who talks about developing these skills, but a teacher who actually provides activities, experiences, and challenges developing the student's hand, heart, mind, and ear in ways that the student can relate to and even love. Students with well-rounded skills are vastly more likely to continue to make music as adults because they can fit into a variety of different musical contexts. Whether it be jamming with their colleagues after work in a rock band, joining the local civic orchestra, or playing Christmas carols at the family holiday party, they will have the skill set to participate confidently in whatever musical endeavors may arise.

9. *Make a Positive Difference*

In the end, this is all that matters. Most teachers will use the above skills to make a difference, but if a teacher can make a positive change in the student some other way, or with some incredible strength in one of the above areas, but a complete absence of the others, then I say, "More power to you."

The Right Teacher
(Not the Perfect Teacher)

As you can see, this is a daunting list, and it doesn't even contain a few logistical necessities such as "show up on time," "maintain a clean, well-lit studio," "communicate with the parent," and "stay in business long enough to make a difference."

The odds that you will find a teacher who is truly excellent in every area are slim to none. Despite years of experience, hours of preparation, and a curriculum based on the latest research and developed with the top teachers in the country, I am frequently disappointed in the quality of my own teaching. In watching my own teaching each week, there are always moments when I catch myself saying something less than helpful or even hurtful in my efforts to improve my students' playing. Or, perhaps I forget to check a crucial assignment or notice a particular moment of excellence. Maybe I was impatient with a student who was doing his absolute best, but still struggling. Maybe, upon reflection, he was struggling because I failed to choose the right music or failed to prepare him for the music I chose.

> The right teacher is someone who effectively works with your family to create a positive learning experience for your child.

Teaching is hard. If it weren't so rewarding, I think I would go find an easier profession. Maybe alligator wrestling.

So, if finding the perfect teacher is impossible, what does it mean to find the "right teacher?"

The right teacher is someone who effectively works with your family to create a positive learning experience for your child. This will be different for each child and each family. My own daughter studies with a Russian conservatory–trained pianist who frequently forgets what she has assigned the previous week and almost never provides performance experiences. She is one of the finest teachers in the world, in my opinion, however, when it comes to developing technique and musicianship, teaching my daughter how to learn on her own, giving clear and honest feedback (both positive and negative), and assessing my daughter's needs. As for remembering the music or providing performance experiences, these are areas our family can effectively provide without any trouble.

You might find that your child is extremely self-driven and critical and therefore needs a teacher who will help her avoid becoming self-destructive. Or perhaps you need a teacher who will provide clear structure and goals because both parents are exceptionally busy, and your child is easygoing and absent-minded but takes criticism well.

Certain aspects of teaching, however, should always be present to an acceptable degree, at the least. For example, in my own case, my early teachers knew very little about developing a solid technical foundation. As a result, an entire year of college had to be devoted to rebuilding my technique, and I am convinced that my pinched nerve, shoulder, elbow, and wrist pain are the result of playing with poor posture and too much tension. While many people may argue that my teachers created in me a sense of joy and passion for music that led me to overcome my technical difficulties, I would argue that there must have been someone better prepared to provide me with the foundation to pursue my dreams without injury (not to sound ungrateful).

Recall what Professor Sophia Gilmson, is fond of saying, "If I could make one rule, it would be this: Only the best teachers are allowed to teach beginners!" A good start is the best assurance of a good ending, my grandmother used to say. So, here are a few tips to finding a good teacher who will work well with your child and your family:

1. Be honest and clear in your assessment of your child's needs and willingness to grow. A good teacher will work with these needs, but also help you understand how you can build systems and learn techniques for making music-learning enjoyable for the whole family.

2. Seek the advice of trained musicians who are also parents. Many parents love their child's teacher despite the fact that their child may be learning next to nothing. In my experience, most parents like teachers who praise their child and create a loving environment. These are all good, but insufficient aspects of teaching. On the other hand, professional musicians are often equally poor judges of excellent teaching. Just because someone is the lead guitarist for your favorite local band or the concertmaster of the symphony does not mean she understands the first thing about how to create an effective learning environment. Musical parents whose children have had successful musical training will often be aware of which teachers are both nurturing and effective.

3. Insist on a trial lesson or trial period, not just a conversation. Observing your child in the context of the lesson is really the only way to judge if this particular teacher will be a good fit for your family. The teacher may come highly recommended, have

terrific results with other children, and be the most nurturing person on the planet, but none of that guarantees he will hit it off with your child.

4. Look for a teacher who will provide clear, written goals both for the week and the year. She should base these goals on the best interests of the child, but also the family situation. For example, a teacher should be interested in the parents' work schedules, the family's travel plans, and so forth, anything that might affect practice time. Of course, it is up to the parent to inform the teacher of these situations.

5. Above all, trust your instincts. A music teacher is often the longest-term mentor a child has. A child will get a new classroom teacher each year (and undoubtedly some of those will be amazing, powerful, and influential), but hopefully she will have the opportunity to work with her music teacher for many years. The teacher need not be perfect, but he should be a source of positive development for your child in as many ways as possible.

APPENDIX B

DELIBERATE PRACTICE FOR THE ADVANCED STUDENT

For the Student's Eyes Only

Note: This section is exclusively for advanced students who are seeking to super-charge their practice. This material is not for parental consumption!

The practice strategies I list here I have learned from my reading about the practice habits of great artists, lessons with some of the greatest teachers in the world, and the research of great educators. Some of them may be useful to you, others a complete waste of time. You must use your own judgment to discover which ones at which times will work best for you.

You are also likely to find that the most effective practice strategies are the most difficult. This is to be expected since the goal is to build new muscles, new neural networks, and new ways of understanding.

Finally, these are simply tools. Like any tool, they are effective only if used with a clear design and intention to create something amazing. Nothing amazing was ever built throwing hammers and wrenches around a work site. You must have a clear idea of what you want, choose the tool that best fits your challenge, and use it wisely.

So that you may diagnose your need and go straight to the area in which you need the most improvement, I have divided the practice strategies into three categories: motivation, musicianship/technique, and learning pieces. Without strategies to become highly motivated, you will not be able to maintain the commitment level needed to engage in the technique and musicianship practice. Without effective technique and musicianship, you will not be able to learn your pieces very well. This is not to say that you should work on these areas one at a time. They are all needed simultaneously if you are to progress and enjoy playing music for a lifetime.

Advanced Practice Strategies for Super-Charging Your Motivation

These strategies were treated briefly as tips for "slump recovery" on pages 121-22. Two of those tips are (1) making a list of all the things you used to love about your instrument and (2) posting a photo that reminds you of your goal where you will see it every day. The rest of the methods are described in greater detail below.

Sign Up for a Scary Goal and Focus on How the Goal Will Change You

When you are ready for it, there is nothing more powerful when it comes to motivation than signing up for a goal that scares you. For me, this was the period between 1996 and 2000, when I entered nearly a dozen music competitions. How well I actually performed in those competitions has had virtually no impact on my career as a musician (even though I won several), but the impact entering those competitions had on my *practice* — and therefore my ability and career — was profound. It wasn't just how much I practiced, but also the way in which I practiced.

I have witnessed this exact same effect on hundreds of students over the years — they sign up for a big benefit concert, they are invited to play at a relative's wedding, or they get a big solo in the church band. At first they are terrified, but then they make a plan, evaluate their progress, and each reaches the goal a changed musician.

Join an Ensemble of Players Better Than You

My jazz guitar teacher in high school, Mimi Fox, used to always tell me, "Make sure you're the worst player in the band. Stretching yourself to play with musicians better than you is the best way to improve." It isn't easy, because you have to somehow convince better players to let you into the group, and you have to deal with the shame and embarrassment that occasionally comes with being the weakest player. Nevertheless, I have always tried to follow her advice because, without a doubt, this is one of the main things that motivated me to focus on eradicating my deficiencies as a musician.

Save Up and Buy a New Instrument

I have a vivid memory of the first time I played each new guitar I have ever owned. There is something profoundly magical about laying your fingers on a new instrument which is a big step up for you. A beautiful instrument inspires everyone who loves music and practically invites us to practice. In addition, a high-quality instrument can inspire us to reach for an equally high quality of playing, while a low-quality instrument can leave us frustrated because no matter how hard we may work, it would be almost impossible to produce a clear, beautiful tone.

Listen to Great Music Every Day

To imagine that we might learn to play music without listening to an immense amount of the finest music we can lay our hands on is like thinking we can learn a language without ever hearing it spoken. All great musicians, from Beethoven to The Beatles, spent thousands of hours immersing themselves in the sounds of their contemporaries. Listen in the car, the shower, while doing homework, and anywhere else when it isn't rude to tune out the people around you. Bathe your entire being in music until it seeps in through your pores.

Go to Concerts

While there's great value in listening to music all the time at home, nothing can ever replace the sound, the feeling, and the excitement of a great live performance. A world-class performer may have the ability to electrify us, teach us, and inspire us to new heights. It is said that the young Johann Sebastian Bach once traveled on foot over 100 miles to witness a performance by the greatest organist of his day. Fortunately, most of us don't have to work that hard to see a great performance.

Take Breaks, but Come Back

It is easy for highly motivated students to think they will make the most progress by pushing themselves relentlessly toward their goal. However, the most successful practicers are more interested in maintaining optimal energy, focus, and cognitive abilities. While top performers have been observed to take breaks every 30 to 60 minutes, it is best to learn to observe our own optimal focus. Some days we may need more frequent breaks; other times we may be on a roll and are able to keep our focus for a longer period. Particularly when it comes to developing the physical skill required to play music, it is better to stop and regenerate than to practice poorly. It is also healthy to take longer periods of time off from playing to recapture our original excitement. After a big performance, for example, most musicians will take a few days off from practice before jumping into learning new repertoire. This time can be used to listen to a wide variety of music and see if there is something that particularly piques our interest or informs our creativity. Alternatively, it can be used to simply rest — mind and body. Too long a break, however, can make it difficult to return to your old form; this can be discouraging, especially to younger students, so I typically do not recommend taking more than one week off from playing. Then, when you return, come back to something you have been excited about playing.

Seasons of Focus

As you may have already noticed, there is far more to learn when becoming an expert than you can ever focus on in a single week, let alone a single day. Between technique, learning new pieces, stage presence, musicianship, listening, composition, ensemble playing, going to concerts, and more, you will never be able to truly dive deeply into a subject if you try to squeeze everything in all at once. Many teachers and students deal with this reality simply by ignoring every area except one or two (usually technique and learning new pieces).

I recommend a different approach for my students, which I call "seasons of focus." One semester we may focus on preparing for a recital, carefully learning and reviewing a dozen of our favorite pieces to perform for an audience. The next semester, we might focus more on composition and music theory. Not that we stop practicing other areas altogether during this period, it's simply that they are no longer our primary focus. In this way, over many years, a student may develop a well-rounded skill set that allows her to excel in all areas.

Advanced Practice Strategies for Improving Your Overall Musical and Technical Ability

In *The 7 Habits of Highly Effective People*, Stephen Covey discusses the concept of production and production capacity. He likens this to the fable of the Goose that Lays Golden Eggs: A king has a goose that lays a golden egg every day, but he gets greedy and kills the goose to get all the eggs out, but then has no goose to lay eggs in the future. Parents and kids both are easily focused on playing harder repertoire sooner rather than building the capacity to play well in a variety of settings in the future. Of course, the opposite can be just as harmful: Always preparing to play well through endless scales and theory will kill your Golden Goose of motivation quicker than a fox in the hen house. As with everything else, talk with your parents and teacher to find the optimal balance for you personally.

Recognize That All Skills Are Interrelated

When you have a weakness in one area, it tends to make all other areas more difficult. Frequently, students will neglect their sight-reading, thinking they only want to be good at playing their favorite pieces. But a student who excels at sight-reading can learn more of his favorite pieces. Other times, a student relies upon his excellent sight-reading but has not trained his ear. A student who has both, however, can hear where the melody is going before he even sees the next measure and prepares his hands and mind for what is coming up.

Train Your Fingers like Little Athletes

Playing music is as much an athletic pursuit as it is an artistic one. Our bodies need strength, flexibility, accuracy, and speed as much as any Olympic gymnast. Seek out the best trainers and employ a rigorous commitment to improving your skills day by day.

Train Your Mind to Recognize Patterns

One of the most common questions we classical musicians hear after a concert is "How do you remember all those notes?!" The truth is, we don't. No one could. We memorize melodies and chord progressions and the form of the piece (how different sections come back at different times) and a variety of other patterns that are common to all music. In fact, the rapid recognition of patterns is one of the principal characteristics that differentiates experts from novices in any field. It is through the rapid "chunking" of large bits of data into known patterns that experts are able to focus their attention on the most important parts and not get overwhelmed by the details. Practicing solfège, rhythm, and music theory will help you to recognize patterns more quickly.

Learn to Improvise and Compose

The creative act of putting notes and rhythms together to form a new piece of music is one of the most challenging and rewarding activities a musician can engage in. It is also, by far, the most effective way to understand music theory. Imagine teaching children to read language, yet never having them write a single story of their own.

For centuries, composing and improvising were simply normal and expected skills for all trained musicians. However, in the late 19th century, there began to be a split between professional composers and professional performers. Many classically trained teachers may find this process intimidating because they themselves are not skilled composers and improvisers. If this is the case with your teacher, don't feel you need to go out and find a new one; simply start messing around on your own, and you might be surprised at what you can create. If you get to a point where you feel you need further assistance, it might be a good idea to add composition or improvisation lessons from a teacher who is an expert in those areas.

Sight-Read Music You Love Daily

Almost all the good sight-readers I know, including myself, went through an extended period of their lives where they read music many hours a day. In all cases I have encountered, they did so not to become better at reading music, but because there was sheet music around that they were interested in playing — maybe it was band, orchestra, or jazz band, a monthly subscription to music magazines with cool pieces in it, or books of their favorite Broadway or pop tunes. Just like learning to read language, reading music is a struggle at first, but if you are introduced to the right material, you fall in love with the stories on the page and can't tear yourself away.

Advanced Practice Strategies for Improving Your Pieces

Every practice technique is like a tool. How you use it is more important than if you use it.

The following strategies are some of the most effective learning techniques used by musicians around the world preparing for high-level performance and competition.

Nevertheless, first note that they can easily be misused. Every practice technique is like a tool. How you use it is more important than if you use it. In my studio, I actually have a pretend toolbox with little paper cutouts of tools, each with a strategy written on it, which I use to explain to my students that it isn't just picking the right tool that is important, it is how you use it. If you are trying to build a tree house, I tell them, you might choose a hammer and nails. But if you start swinging the hammer around wildly or throwing the nails at the tree, it is unlikely you will have a tree house any time soon. Similarly, you can choose to practice slowly, but if you are thinking about Minecraft while slowly playing half the notes incorrectly, it is unlikely you will make much progress on your piece.

1. *Super-Slow Practice*

This practice is universally recommended by all great teachers in both music and sports for a good reason: It works. The slower the better. Some teachers even recommend playing so slowly that the music becomes completely unrecognizable. For children (and many adults), this kind of practice is excruciatingly boring, which is why you need either to be extremely motivated or make it into a game.

2. *Add-On from the End*

When practicing, most of us have an unfortunate tendency to play from the beginning until we hit a hard spot or make a mistake, struggle with that problem, then start over from the beginning, and see if we can make it through. The result, over many days, weeks, and possibly months of practice, is that we end up vastly more secure with the beginning of the piece than we are with the end. In addition, in this sort of practice, we are always playing into unknown territory, and thus naturally become more tense and insecure as we play.

An alternative approach is to learn the very end of the piece first, and then learn the phrase before the end, then the phrase before that, and so on, until we reach the beginning. Because there is no more music after the end of the piece, we are not tempted to continue playing sections we have not securely learned. Because this approach can make it so difficult to fully grasp the composer's intent, I usually begin by listening to recordings, then sight-reading through the piece as best I can, and once I feel I understand how the piece is supposed to go, I begin learning it from the end in earnest. One way to visualize this type of practice would be to imagine learning the alphabet by adding one letter at a time starting with the letter "Z," such that we would say, "Z," "Y-Z," "X-Y-Z," etc.

3. *Slow-Fast Practice*

Often described as dotted rhythm practice by trained musicians, this is simply a way to take a passage of fast notes and play the first note slowly and the second fast, in this pattern: slow, fast, slow, fast, slow, fast, etc. When it is mastered, you simply reverse the order, making the first note fast, the second slowly, and so on. This allows you to practice speed without building up tension.

4. *Metronome Practice*

Many students and teachers misunderstand the true benefit of the metronome. Some think it is a way to force yourself to play faster by keeping up with the metronome. Others think it is a way to force yourself to play with a steady beat. In my experience, if you're having trouble playing fast enough or keeping a steady beat, it is either because there is a technical impediment — such is a wrong fingering, too much tension, poorly learned notes or shifts — or any of a million possible problems that have nothing to do with an annoying ticking gadget.

Nevertheless, I find metronome practice to be one of the most useful practice techniques ever invented. This is mostly because the metronome can help you play a difficult passage extremely slowly (see practice technique #1) and then gradually increase the speed in such small increments that the mind and body hardly even notice. I remember thinking that the metronome had an almost magical effect on my playing when I first began following my teacher's suggestion. Once I had the fingerings, notes, and rhythms, all I had to do was set the metronome to a speed that made the passage easy, then repeat the passage at a pace one click faster, again and again until I reached the desired tempo. The magic was that I could put even the most impossibly difficult passages through this process and within 10 to 15 minutes be able to play them comfortably.

5. Solve One Problem at a Time, Completely and Securely

The definition of focus is concentrating on one thing at a time. Unfortunately, a difficult piece of music may throw us half a dozen curveballs in the span of just a few notes: We may need to shift our arm while curving our finger to precisely the right angle, plucking three strings, all the while perfectly executing a delicate diminuendo. Oftentimes, because we are in a hurry, we feel we don't have time to practice each of these separate challenges, if we are even aware of them as separate challenges in the first place. As I often say to my students, however, "The slow way is the fast way." What I mean by this is that by taking just a little bit of time to understand and master each of the small challenges before putting them back together to create a single fluid movement, we can often save ourselves hours of practice, struggling to overcome problems that have now become habituated.

6. *Start from Anywhere*

This is more of a performance preparation strategy than a learning strategy, but forcing yourself to start from any place in the music is a great way to test if you really know the piece. Furthermore, this approach will undoubtedly reveal weaknesses you had skimmed over and may even reveal hidden gems in the music you previously had not noticed.

7. *Creative Problem-Solving*

Far too often, students seem to believe it is their job to beat their heads mindlessly against the music and wait until their lesson day for their teacher to offer a creative solution.

Not only are most difficult problems solved with at least some amount of creative thinking (and, of course, a lot of hard work), but the sheer joy of discovering your own way to play a passage is one of the best parts of practice. The trick is to keep an open mind and a willingness to try anything — even the ridiculous.

> *MUSIC LESSON TO LIFE LESSON*
> Don't cut corners; by giving the small details adequate attention up front, you save yourself the headache of having to spend more time fixing things down the line.

Most important of all, write your ideas down! I can't begin to tell you how often I have come up with a new fingering or interpretation and then been unable to practice for a day or two, only to completely forget what passage I had been working on before. The two seconds it takes to make a note of your idea will save you hours of frustration later.

> *MUSIC LESSON TO LIFE LESSON*
> One-size does not fit all; no one knows your unique strengths and weaknesses better than you, so who better, then, to come up with a creative solution to a practice rut?

8. *Begin with the End in Mind*

One study of practicing musicians found that advanced players took more time to envision how they wanted the music to go prior to beginning to learn it than less-experienced players did.

MUSIC LESSON TO LIFE LESSON
If you have a clear roadmap of where you are going, you can make a more effective plan to get there.

---

9. *Record Yourself and Listen Back*

Listening to a recording of yourself playing is, for most people, like fingernails on a chalkboard — in other words, uncomfortable at best. However, there is no better way to truly know how we sound. For this strategy to be truly effective, it is best while listening back to make notes in the score about what we need to improve. When I'm at my absolute best, I record myself at the end of my practice and listen back at the start of my practice the next day, making notes to inform my practice that day. Nowadays, most people have half-a-dozen devices at home that can create a high-quality recording. My recommendation is to be sure to listen back through *speakers* rather than on your phone so that you can get a truer representation of the sound of your playing.

10. *Mental Practice*

A study of basketball players found that alternating periods of visualizing shooting a basketball from the free-throw line and actually practicing shooting free throws yielded faster improvement than practicing with a basketball alone.

The ability to sit quietly and visualize every note, every movement, and every expressive device of a passage or piece of music is one of the most powerful, and at the same time agonizingly difficult, practice strategies. As we discussed, however, all the real training takes place in the brain. So, it makes sense that concentrating on firing the neural pathways involved in performing the piece of music would yield the fastest improvement on that piece of music.

ഇ

Now you have a very full toolbox, from which you can discover the tools that work best for you. I wish you a happy musical journey!

BIBLIOGRAPHY

Bloom, Benjamin S., ed. *Developing Talent in Young People*. Ballantine Books, 1985.

Duke, Robert A. *Intelligent Music Teaching*. Learning and Behavior Resources, 2009.

Duke, Robert A., et al. "It's Not How Much; It's How," *Journal of Research in Music Education*, vol. 56, no. 4, 2009, pp. 310-21.

Dweck, Dr. Carol. *Mindset: The New Psychology of Success*. Ballantine Books, 2006.

Gilbert, Daniel T., and Jane E. J. Ebert. "Decisions and Revisions: The Affective Forecasting of Changeable Outcomes," *Journal of Personality and Social Psychology*, 2002.

Kodály, Zoltán. *The Selected Writings of Zoltán Kodály*. Boosey & Hawkes, 1974.

Laditan, Bunmi. "How to Be a Mom in 2017," post. Bunmi Laditan Facebook Fan Page, May 1, 2017, https://www.facebook.com/BunmiKLaditan/posts/how-to-be-a-mom-in-2017-make-sure-your-childrens-academic-emotional-psychologica/1899244270322560/.

National Research Council. *How People Learn*. National Academies Press, 2000.

Schwartz, Barry. *The Paradox of Choice: Why More Is Less*. Harper Collins, 2004.

"Teens and Sleep." *National Sleep Foundation,* 2019, www.sleepfound-ation.org/articles/teens-and-sleep.

Thaler, Richard. "People Aren't Dumb. The World Is Hard." Interview with Stephen J. Dubner. *Freakonomics Radio,* episode 340, Stitcher and Dubner Productions, 11 July 2018, freakonomics.com/podcast/richard-thaler/.

ABOUT THE AUTHOR

Dr. Klondike Steadman

An award-winning guitarist, Klondike also shares his passion for music as an educator, entrepreneur, and author. Klondike founded the Educational Outreach Program in 2001 as an outgrowth of the Austin Classical Guitar Society. The low-income high-school students who receive expert, private, free guitar instruction in this program go on to give public concerts regularly as soloists and in guitar ensembles.

In 2003, Klondike received the prestigious Studio Fellowship Award from the Music Teachers National Association and launched the Orpheus Academy of Music with his wife, Wendy Kuo. As the co-founder and director, he has built one of the most successful and innovative music programs for kids in the country. In addition to his line of method books, *The Complete Guitar*, he has also collaborated with Orpheus Academy faculty to create an approach to private music instruction called *Adventures Through Sound* that uses singing, movement, and folk songs to teach guitar and piano students.

Among the many students Klondike has taught over the years who continue to make music as adults, several have won prizes in national competitions, been accepted to prestigious music departments, and gone on to significant music careers in classical, popular, and folk genres. But these accomplishments are no more significant than those who have formed bands with friends, play regularly at church, or just play to relax after a hard day at work.

Lightning Source UK Ltd.
Milton Keynes UK
UKHW022021170720
366727UK00014B/172